Convicted to Grow

Rebuild Your Confidence and Rise Stronger

By

Tressa Manns

Published by **Convicted to Grow Coaching, LLC**
www.tressamanns.com | www.convictedtogrowcoaching.com

ISBN: **979-8-218-70993-8**

Printed in the United States of America

First Edition: 2025

Acknowledgments

Writing this book has been a rebuilding journey and a bold declaration of growth. I could not have rebuilt or risen stronger without the people who believed in me, poured into me, and stood with me in every season of becoming.

To God who is FIRST in everything that I do – Thank You for being my source. For turning my pain into purpose, and for giving me strength when I had none left. You've carried me through it all.

To my late significant other – Your love lives in me. Losing you changed everything—but your memory gave me the courage to start again. You were the spark behind my rebuild.

To my family – Thank you for being patient with my process, and present in my healing and growth journey. Your quiet strength, your prayers, and your belief in me never went unnoticed.

To my friends, mentors, and inner circle – You saw me at my lowest and still reminded me who I was. Thank you for the pep talks, truth-telling, and unconditional love.

To the **Lion's Behavior Community** and the **Convicted to Grow Community**—thank you for more than just your belief in me. You held me accountable, supported me through every draft, every doubt, and every breakthrough. You didn't just cheer me on—you stood in the gap, reminded me of the mission, and reminded me to keep going.

To every reader holding this book – Thank you for choosing yourself. Thank you for doing the work. I hope these words reminded you of your power, and that it's never too late to rebuild.

This book is for anyone who's been knocked down, but refused to stay there. For those convicted to grow, no matter what. I'm honored to walk this journey with you.

With deep gratitude,

— Coach Tressa

Table of Contents

Part I:
The Fall

Introduction

The phrase *Convicted to Grow* is more than just a title—it's a call to action. It embodies a mindset—a deep, unwavering commitment to personal growth, no matter the obstacles. These words didn't just come to me; they emerged from my journey of setbacks, reinvention, and rebuilding my confidence. In this book, I'll show you how to adopt this conviction in your own life so you too can rise stronger, step into your purpose, and rebuild your confidence.

As a professional, a leader, or an aspiring entrepreneur, you have likely faced moments when life knocked you down—whether through career setbacks, business failures, personal loss, or simply feeling stuck and unfulfilled. These challenges can feel like roadblocks, but they don't have to define you.

After facing major setbacks, including the loss of my significant other and a career that drained me emotionally and physically, I found myself at a place where I no longer recognized who I was. I had spent years chasing success, doing everything I was "supposed" to do, yet still felt lost. The fire that once fueled me had gone out. I had to make a choice: let the pain define me or use it as fuel to rise. I chose to rise and rebuild my confidence, step by step.

This book is about making a powerful shift: from surviving to thriving, from feeling stuck and lost to stepping into clarity, confidence, and success. Setbacks are not endings—they are opportunities for reinvention and growth. You are convicted to grow.

This was my moment to rebuild, reinvent, and rise into the person I was truly meant to be. I had to reclaim my confidence, find my voice, and redefine success on my own terms. I became convicted to growing. I embraced daily personal growth, leaned into resilience, and learned what it meant to thrive despite life's hardest setbacks. Now, as a motivational speaker, confidence and business strategy coach, and leader, I'm here to show you that you can do the same.

Action Item: Your Convicted to Grow Notebook

Before you dive into this transformational journey, make a commitment—not to me, but to yourself. This book is filled with action steps, reflections, and mindset shifts that will require you to be intentional. To get the most out of this experience, I encourage you to get a notebook dedicated solely to this journey. Document your thoughts, breakthroughs, and respond to the reflection prompts as you move forward in your journey.

Here's what to do:

1. **Find a notebook**—one that you'll use specifically for this journey. Make it special, something that represents a fresh start.

2. **Title it "Convicted to Grow."** Let this serve as your personal guide to transformation.

3. **On the first page, write and sign this commitment statement:**

   I am committed to my personal and professional growth. I choose to rebuild, reinvent, and elevate myself, no matter the setbacks I face. I will use this notebook to document my reflections, lessons, and action steps as I take ownership of my journey. My growth starts now.

4. **Date it.** This marks the beginning of your growth journey.

5. **Use this notebook throughout the book.** Each chapter will include action steps and exercises—this is where you'll reflect, set goals, and track your progress.

You are not just reading this book—you are actively stepping into your next level. This is where you start making the changes that will transform your life. Let's get started.

How You'll Digest This Book

This book is designed to take you on a clear, structured path of growth. Each part builds on the previous one, guiding you step-by-step through your transformation. Here's how the journey is broken down:

Part One: The Fall

This is where the journey begins—acknowledging the moment everything fell apart. Whether it was grief, burnout, or losing your sense of self, this section helps you sit with the reality of your setback while showing you that it doesn't define you. You'll begin to shift your thinking, start reclaiming your confidence, and prepare to rise.

Part Two: The Rebuild

Now that you've faced the fall, it's time to rise. This section is about rebuilding what you lost—starting with your confidence. You'll reconnect with your voice, realign with your purpose, and begin to take back your power in life, business, and leadership. You'll learn to believe in your own strength once again and reclaim your life's narrative.

Part Three: The Rise

In this phase, you'll stop surviving and start expanding. It's about building new habits, strengthening your mindset, and stepping into your next level with intentional growth. You'll learn how to show up as a leader and elevate your life with purpose, with a newfound belief in your ability to rise to the challenge.

Part Four: The Commitment

This is where transformation becomes a lifestyle. You'll learn how to stay resilient when life throws curveballs, define success on your own terms, and stay grounded in the conviction to keep growing. This is your foundation for sustainable success, purpose, and legacy—built on unshakable confidence and the conviction to keep going.

You'll learn how to stay resilient when life throws curveballs, define success on your own terms, and stay grounded in the conviction to keep growing. This is your foundation for sustainable success, purpose, and legacy—built on unshakable confidence and the conviction to keep going.

How This Approach Helps You

The path to growth doesn't have to be overwhelming. This structure is intentionally laid out to keep you moving forward with purpose:

- Step-by-step progression so you can take it one phase at a time, ensuring you never feel rushed or overwhelmed.
- Action steps at the end of each chapter to help you immediately apply the lessons you've learned to your life and career.
- A mix of storytelling and strategy, designed to keep you engaged, motivated, and empowered to keep going.

This book isn't just my story—it's your story. It's about shifting your mindset, rebuilding your confidence, and elevating your life. If you've ever felt stuck, lost, or unsure of what's next, this book will give you the tools, strategies, and mindset shifts to help you rebuild and thrive in your life, career, and business. You're not just surviving—you're ready to rise. This is your time to reclaim your confidence and step into your next level of growth.

Chapter 1:
The Power of Acknowledging Setbacks

The Moment That Changed Everything

Uncertainty has this sneaky way of trapping us, making us feel undeserving and devoid of any value as if the future holds nothing in store for us. I can personally attest that temporary setbacks are an inevitable part of life's journey. Each person's journey is unique, and while what may be a setback for you might not relate to the setbacks I've experienced, it doesn't make them any less impactful.

On November 8, 2022 at 12:25am, I lost my fiancé. to a sudden heart attack. That same year, I faced the heartbreaking loss of other beloved individuals: my grandma, my uncle. Among these profound losses, the death of my partner hit me the hardest. The grief was all-consuming. It was unexpected and there were no warning signs that day before that would be his last day enjoying and riding his motorcycle followed by his last dinner that he made. After ten months of deep sorrow but weekly therapy, I knew it was time to embrace my new reality and chart a fresh course—especially as I turned 45 the following year.

So yes, 2022 was a pivotal year—one that catapulted me into my conviction and purpose. Just before my partner's passing, I had made the difficult decision to step away from my high demanding executive leadership role. Burnout had taken a serious toll on my health, and I found myself in Urgent Care, overwhelmed and exhausted. I'll never forget the doctor looking me in the eye and saying with a firm, unwavering tone: "You need to take time off—or this stress is going to kill you."

With that wake-up call—and my partner's blessing and encouragement—I walked away, believing I was being called to something greater. I felt a deep pull toward the entrepreneurial journey, to use my voice to change lives as a speaker and coach. I envisioned 2022 as the year I would fully embrace that purpose, thriving and sharing my gifts with the world. But life had other plans.

His sudden passing sent me into a whirlwind of grief and uncertainty. If I had known what was coming, maybe I would have clung to the familiarity of my 9-5 job, avoiding the pain that followed. Still, that season of "what's next?" became one of the most transformative chapters of my life. Because even in our darkest moments, there's a path forward we don't always see—and it's in walking that path that I found the conviction I now carry every single day.

The reality is, I never saw any of it coming. One moment, I was thriving in my career, deeply engaged, and building a future that included the dream of financially securing my parents' retirement. The next moment, I was engulfed in grief and struggling to find my way back to a healthy version of myself. Burnout had already taken a toll, manifesting in weight gain, anxiety, and a deep sense of depression that left me feeling like I'd lost myself entirely. It's easy to lose sight of who we are and what truly makes us happy when we're suffering in silence, afraid to voice our biggest dreams. But dreams remain dreams until we take bold steps to make them reality, and I knew that to get to where I am today, I had to push through the pain, burnout and identity loss. Burnout was my wake-up call. It forced me to reevaluate everything I thought success meant. That bold decision to walk away was the first spark that began reigniting who I really was.

I could have put on a façade, pretending everything was fine, but a small voice inside kept telling me that my story wasn't just for me— it was meant to inspire and empower others. I didn't see it then, but now, as this book comes to life, I understand that every moment of struggle was shaping me to fulfill my purpose.

I've truly learned the value of gratitude for the little things in life. Being able to wake up every single morning and freely walk around, having the sun shining down on me, all the while hearing the birds chirping is a blessing. When he passed away (God rest his soul), it stirred something deep within me. It made me realize that as long as I'm here on God's green earth, I should always be growing and striving to be the best version of myself.

Being in a place filled with agitation, anger, frustration, and bitterness—being in a place where the fruit of the spirit is absent, hinders us from becoming the best versions of who we truly are. You know, I thought I knew myself, but the truth is, I've always been a reflection of what everybody else wanted me to be and do. I was constantly pouring into others while silently depleting myself, navigating my grief behind a well-crafted mask. On the outside, I looked accomplished and happy, but inside, I was crumbling. I had mastered the art of "faking it till you make it," wearing a brave face while suffering in silence. But that silent suffering was slowly eroding my joy, purpose, and peace.

Here's the thing about grief: it's not just emotional; it's physical, mental, and spiritual. It seeps into every part of your being, weighing you down in ways you never imagined possible. Grief is more than losing a loved one; it comes in many forms. You can lose your career unexpectedly, your home to foreclosure, your car to repossession, a relationship to divorce or breakup, or even lose your identity along the way. Grief leaves a void that demands acknowledgment and healing, and along the way, it can erode your confidence. When you lose something or someone foundational, you start to question your own strength and direction. I tried to keep pushing through, throwing myself into busy work, hoping that if I stayed busy enough, the void would fade. But instead, I found myself lost, exhausted, and disconnected from the life I once envisioned. Rebuilding my confidence meant acknowledging that void, understanding that grief was part of my journey, and finding the strength to rise again.

Acknowledging the Setback, but Not Staying Stuck

Acknowledgment is the cornerstone of any true rebuilding journey. Until we face our setbacks head-on, we remain stuck in a cycle of denial and numbness that prevents growth. I know firsthand how easy it is to get lost in that haze—when I was grieving, I was numb, and that numbness held me hostage. It kept me from stepping into my purpose and showing up for those who needed me. The moment I acknowledged my pain and my setbacks, I unlocked the door to healing and growth. It's in that acknowledgment that we find the courage to move forward, to break free from the chains of the past, and to start rebuilding a life aligned with our true purpose. Acknowledgment is the first step in transforming setbacks into stepping stones on the path to a more empowered and purposeful life.

One of the hardest parts of dealing with a setback—whether in your career, business, finances, relationships, or personal growth—is feeling like you have lost control. The uncertainty, the frustration, and even the disappointment can be overwhelming. It's easy to fall into the cycle of asking, "Why did this happen to me?"

I understand. I asked myself that question countless times.

But here's what I learned: The moment you stop resisting your reality and start acknowledging it, you regain power. Avoiding failure, rejection, or burnout only prolongs suffering. Instead, you have to sit with it, process it, and then choose to move forward with a renewed mindset.

One of the biggest reasons we get stuck is self-doubt. There were moments on this journey of growth and building where I questioned if I was good enough to be a speaker or a coach. I told myself I wasn't fully healed, and that made me doubt my purpose. But here's what I've learned: going through challenges doesn't change who you're meant to be or the destiny you're called to fulfill. Setbacks are just setups for comebacks.

When I first stepped into speaking and coaching a few years back, I worried about how I could help others when I wasn't fully healed myself. But healing is a personal journey, and no one else can dictate your timeline. I realized that sharing my story—my grief, my setbacks, and my journey—wasn't a sign of weakness but of strength. My authenticity, being real and raw, resonated with people. It showed them that I, too, had to overcome self-doubt and fear of failure.

Today, I embrace my growth journey fully. I'm not ashamed of my story—it's what's put me on stages and connected me with others. People don't want fluff; they want the real journey of how to rise again. And that's what I deliver—freeing myself from self-doubt, fear, and overthinking so I can help others do the same. Embracing this growth journey has transformed me, and I'm all in.

Here's what helped me shift my thinking:

- **Acknowledge the setback:** Whether it's losing a job, a failed business, or feeling like you're at a crossroads, recognize what happened without judgment. Accept that the past cannot be changed, but your response to it can be.

- **Recognize what is in your control:** You may not be able to change the setback itself, but you can control your next steps, how you perceive the situation, and how you prepare for what's ahead.

- **Reframe the question:** Instead of asking, "Why me?" start asking, "What's next?" This simple shift in mindset moves you from victimhood to ownership.

- **Let go of perfection:** Setbacks often make us feel like we've failed, but failure is just part of the process. Growth is messy. Progress is never a straight line.

Shifting from 'Why Me?' to 'What's Next?'

There comes a moment when staying stuck in the past no longer serves us. For me, that moment came when I released the guilt of moving forward. I realized my partner would have wanted me to thrive—not just survive.

So, I started asking myself these crucial questions:

- What lessons can I learn from this experience?
- Who do I want to become in this new chapter?
- What does rebuilding my life look like?

Rebuilding after loss, burnout, or any major life shift isn't about forgetting the past—it's about using it as fuel for your next chapter.

The Reality of Setbacks: We All Face Them

At some point, we all face moments that shake us—whether it's losing a job, watching a business fail, dealing with a toxic work environment, struggling financially, or navigating personal hardships. These moments can feel overwhelming, but they are not meant to break you; they are meant to build you.

A setback is not the end of your story—it's the beginning of a new chapter. However, the way you respond to setbacks determines whether you stay stuck in frustration or move forward with power. Do you see obstacles as barriers, or as stepping stones to something greater?

The first step in overcoming any setback is acceptance. You cannot change what happened, but you can control how you move forward.

Setbacks have a way of showing you just how resilient you really are. They remind you that success isn't always a straight line—and sometimes the detour is where the real transformation happens. They teach you that an ending isn't the end—it's just making space for what's next. And even when it feels like you've lost yourself, you haven't. You're being refined. I didn't just survive my setback—I grew through it. That pain shaped me, stretched me, and helped me rise stronger. I wouldn't be the woman, the speaker, or the coach I am today without it. And if you hear nothing else, hear this: you can grow through what you never thought you'd get through.

When I reflect on my journey, especially the falls I've faced, I realize I wouldn't be where I am today without those setbacks. My days of weariness, the moments of anxiety, and even the times I found myself in a state of depression—all of it was part of the process. I had to acknowledge that it's okay not to be okay. The purpose inside me was bigger than my circumstances, and I had to remind myself that falling doesn't mean staying down. It means taking the steps—no matter how small—to rise and rebuild.

Looking back, it took a lot. Yes, I went through months of therapy. Yes, I joined communities for accountability. Yes, there were countless days of prayer and meditation when it was just me and God. But all of that was necessary for growth. It was crucial for the journey.

Even when I didn't feel confident in becoming a coach or a speaker, there was a voice inside me that said, "Yes, you can." But first, I had to acknowledge where I was so I could recalibrate and shift into who I was meant to be.

Why Do We Get Stuck? The Mindset Blocks Holding You Back

When facing major life transitions, many of us get trapped in cycles of:

- **Self-doubt:** "Maybe I'm not good enough to move forward."
- **Fear of failure:** "What if I try again and fail?"
- **Blame and resentment:** "This isn't fair—why is this happening to me?"
- **Paralysis by overthinking:** "I don't know what to do next, so I'll just stay here."

The problem with these thoughts? They keep you stuck. Growth cannot happen in a place of fear and hesitation. It happens when you shift from asking "Why me?" to asking "What's next?"

Instead of viewing setbacks as failures, start seeing them as:

- **A Redirection:** What if this challenge is pushing you toward a better opportunity?
- **A Reset:** What if this is your chance to pause, reassess, and realign with your true goals?
- **A Rebuild:** What if this is the perfect time to reinvent yourself in life, career, or business?

I had to make this shift myself. After losing my partner and leaving my career, I had two choices: stay stuck in pain or turn my situation into power. Once I changed my mindset, everything else changed.

If you're reading this and you've been feeling stuck—whether in your career, business, or personal life—this is your wake-up call. You don't have to have all the answers, but you do have to make the decision to move forward.

Instead of viewing setbacks as failures, we need to see them as opportunities for redirection, a reset, and a chance to rebuild stronger than before. When life throws you off course, it's not a dead end—it's a detour guiding you to a path you might not have considered. Just like I had to choose between staying stuck in grief and burnout or turning my pain into power, every setback is a pivotal moment. It's a signal to pause, reassess, and come back even stronger. Setbacks teach us resilience, refine our purpose, and ultimately shape us into who we're meant to become. So, embrace those moments, because they aren't the end of your story—they're the chapters that make your comeback even more powerful.

We shouldn't be ashamed of our setbacks because they are the very chapters that shape our resilience and fuel our purpose. Often, I see clients hesitant to share their struggles—whether it's losing a job, facing a breakup, or enduring a traumatic experience. But what I've learned is that those very setbacks are the testimony that inspires others. When we own our stories, we transform them into powerful messages of hope. I've faced everything from grief, burnout, and financial struggles to sleeping in my car and surviving abusive relationships. I'm not ashamed to share any of it because it's those experiences that turned my pain into my platform. They let others see that if I can rise from those ashes, so can they. By sharing our setbacks, we not only free ourselves but also empower others to step boldly into their own calling. It's not about what we've been through—it's about how we've overcome and who we've become in the process.

Final Thoughts

You may not have chosen your setback, but you get to choose your comeback. Your story isn't over. It's just being rewritten with strength, clarity, and purpose. Don't wait until you "feel ready" to start rebuilding. Start where you are—with your truth, your resilience, and your voice. You're not behind. You're becoming. You are not broken. You are being rebuilt—bolder, wiser, and more powerful than before.

Action Steps: Own the Setback- Then Shift

To reclaim your power and move forward, begin with these steps:

- **Tell the Truth About the Setback.**
  Write it down—what happened, how it impacted you, and what you've been carrying silently. Stop sugarcoating your struggle. Healing starts with honesty.

- **Identify the Trigger Moments.**
  What moments made you feel like you lost control, confidence, or clarity? Pinpoint them. Clarity creates awareness—and awareness creates the power to shift.

- **Release the Shame.**

  Setbacks are not a sign of failure—they're part of the process. Write this down and repeat it until you believe it:

  "My setback didn't break me. It revealed what I'm made of."

- **Reframe the Story.**

  What lessons are hidden in what you went through? Grab your journal and write a new narrative:

  "Because of that moment, I've grown in..." (Confidence, courage, clarity—you name it.)

- **Take Back the Pen.**

  You're the author of what comes next. What's one action you can take this week to stop shrinking and start rebuilding—personally, professionally, or emotionally?

- **Commit to a Small Step Forward.**

  You're the author of what comes next. What's one action you can take this week to stop shrinking and start rebuilding—personally, professionally, or emotionally?

Chapter 2:
Breaking Free from Fear and Overcoming Imposter Syndrome

Before you can rebuild or elevate anything in your life, you have to confront what's been silently holding you back. Not the circumstances, not other people—but the beliefs that have been running on autopilot in your mind. The ones that whisper, *"You're not good enough"*, *"Who do you think you are?"*, *"You're too late."* Those voices? They've been lying to you.

For years, I wore a mask of confidence. I showed up at work, managed people, delivered results, made the company a lot of money and checked all the boxes. On the outside, I was the go-to person. But inside, I questioned my worth. I second-guessed my ideas, hesitated to speak up, and dismissed compliments. I overworked myself to prove I belonged—especially as the only minority woman in a leadership role. I felt I had to make sure I rose to my best even when I felt like I was stretched thin and working 12-16 hour days.

At the peak of my corporate leadership career, holding the highest position I had ever achieved, I realized that my next move needed to be my best move. Despite the fear and uncertainty, I knew that the burnout and the toll on my health signaled it was time to take a leap of faith. This decision wasn't made lightly; it was the result of countless days and nights wrestling with the realization that to truly pivot into my gifts and step into my purpose, I had to embrace change.

As 2022 approached, I knew this leap was necessary for me to become the woman I am today, fully aligned with my purpose and potential.

And when I left that career—burned out and pretty much losing myself—I realized how loud the inner critic had become. Without the title, without the corporate validation, I felt like I had nothing left. The self-doubt grew louder: *"You're starting over at this age? Who's going to listen to you now?"* I had to get honest with myself. The job wasn't the only thing I needed to leave behind—I had to let go of the mental chains too.

Identifying the Limiting Beliefs

The first step to silencing self-doubt is identifying the beliefs you've been carrying—and where they came from. Limiting beliefs don't just show up one day. They're often rooted in:

- Childhood experiences
- Past failures or disappointments
- Cultural or societal expectations
- Toxic work environments or relationships
- Comparison to others in real life or on social media

These beliefs become the silent scripts that shape how we see ourselves and what we believe is possible.Here are a few of the most common lies that keep us stuck:

- "I'm not good enough."
- "If I try, I'll probably fail again."
- " My voice doesn't matter. "
- "It has to be perfect before I start it."
- "Other people are better at this than me."
- "What if I fail?]"
- "No one will take me seriously."

Sound familiar? These beliefs are not facts—they're fears and you have the power to rewrite them. The truth is: you are more capable than you've been led to believe.

For me, one of my deepest beliefs was that I had to earn my worth through performance. If I wasn't constantly producing, proving, or pleasing, I felt invisible. I now know that my value isn't tied to what I do, but who I am.

The fear of failure loomed large as I contemplated leaving my corporate role. What if I didn't succeed as a full-time entrepreneur? What if this bold move ended in failure and forced me to return to the corporate world? It's natural to fear taking such a leap, especially when you have family and other commitments to consider. For me, being an empty nester made the choice somewhat easier, yet the haunting question remained: what if I failed? The thought of not succeeding and facing the embarrassment of returning to my old path was daunting.

Ultimately, I had to silence those doubts and tell myself that this move had to work. There was no room for self-doubt or fear of losing because I had reached a stage where burnout had stripped away my motivation. I wasn't inspired to lead or show up as my best self. Burnout had clouded my life with frustration and aggravation, affecting not only me but those around me. It was time to step out of that shadow and truly commit to showing up as the best version of myself.

The Impact of Fear and Imposter Syndrome

Fear disguises itself as caution, whispering 'play it safe.' It tricks you into thinking it's protecting you, but in reality, it's holding you back from stepping into your true potential. The key to growth is moving forward despite the fear. It tells you that your accomplishments don't matter, that you're a fraud, and that one day people will "find you out."

I've experienced imposter syndrome even while leading teams, coaching clients, and speaking on stages. I'd walk off stage after delivering a message that moved people—messages I knew came from a place of truth and purpose—only to sit backstage and question if I said enough, if I made sense, if I truly deserved the applause. That's what imposter syndrome does—it robs you of your right-now joy by making you question your right to be in the room.

It makes you shrink in spaces where you were meant to shine. It convinces you that you're not ready, even when you've been called. It attaches conditions to your worth—"once you get that certification, once you have more experience, once someone validates you." But here's the truth: you are already enough. Not someday. Now.

Confidence isn't the absence of fear. It's the decision to move forward in spite of it. It's choosing to believe in your voice—even when it trembles. It's knowing that you don't have to feel ready to be ready.

Imposter Syndrome: When You Feel Like You Don't Belong

Imposter syndrome is the inner voice that whispers, "Who do you think you are?" It's the feeling of being a fraud, even when you've worked hard and earned your place.

It happens to professionals, leaders, and entrepreneurs at every level—even the most successful people in the world experience it.

What I've learned in my 20+ years of combined corporate leadership, coaching, and speaking is that so many of us have faced imposter syndrome at some point in our lives. Whether it's in our 9-to-5 jobs, presenting in the boardroom, or stepping into new roles, or leaping into full time entrepreneurship, imposter syndrome doesn't discriminate. However, I've noticed it's especially prevalent among women, particularly in male-dominated industries. Women often feel they have to strive for perfection or prove their worthiness, sometimes leading them to silence their voices and go with the flow just to fit in.

I've experienced imposter syndrome numerous times, especially in environments where I was the only minority woman in executive leadership. Surrounded by men with impressive credentials and lengthy resumes, it was easy to feel like I was merely a token of diversity rather than a leader in my own right. I'd question whether I belonged, if I was saying the right things, or if I was good enough to hold that position. Imposter syndrome would sneak in and overshadow my accomplishments, making me forget that I was chosen for my expertise and leadership.

Imposter syndrome makes you feel like you don't belong—even when you've earned your place. It tricks you into thinking you're a fraud, even after years of experience. But you don't need more validation; you are already enough. It makes you question your skills, downplay your achievements, and feel like at any moment, someone will "find out" you're not as capable as they think. Sound familiar? This sneaky form of self-doubt doesn't just show up when you're starting something new—it can creep in even after years of experience, making you hesitate to charge your worth, apply for that promotion, or confidently own your expertise. The problem isn't that you aren't qualified—it's that you don't *feel* like you are. But here's what I need you to know: you don't need more degrees, more validation, or more permission. You are already enough. The key to overcoming imposter syndrome is recognizing that those doubts are just noise. You've worked for this. You *are* capable. And it's time to step up and own it.

Breaking Free from Fear and Self-Doubt

When I first started my journey as a speaker and coach, I battled imposter syndrome. I questioned if people would listen to me, if my experiences were valid, or if I was truly "qualified" to lead others.

One day, after a speaking engagement, a woman approached me and said, "Your story changed my perspective. I didn't realize I needed to hear this today." That moment made me realize something: It was never about me. It was about the people who needed what I had to offer. That's the thing about fear—it tricks you into focusing on yourself rather than the people you are meant to serve, impact, and inspire.

Fear is a dream killer. It keeps you stuck in your comfort zone, playing it safe, and second-guessing every decision. It whispers, *What if you fail? What if they judge you? What if you're not ready?*—and before you know it, you're standing still while opportunities pass you by. Fear will have you overthinking instead of taking action, settling instead of striving, and watching others succeed while you sit on the sidelines. Whether it's the fear of failure, rejection, or the unknown, it creates invisible barriers that keep you from reaching your full potential. But here's the truth: fear will always be there, but it doesn't have to control you. Growth happens when you feel the fear and do it anyway. The moment you push past it, you realize it was never as powerful as you thought.

I remember staring at the resignation letter for weeks, my heart racing every time I thought about submitting it. What if I failed? What if this dream of coaching and speaking didn't work out? Fear had me stuck, making me believe that security was better than purpose. But the moment I chose to trust myself, everything shifted. Was it easy? No. But fear lost its power the moment I took action.

Rewiring the Mindset: From Self-Doubt to Self-Belief

Reclaiming your confidence starts with reprogramming your internal dialogue.

Here are the steps I used to shift from fear to faith in myself:

- **Catch the lie.** Start paying attention to the thoughts that replay in your mind. When you hear the inner critic say, *"You're not good enough,"* pause and question it.

- **Challenge the belief.** Ask yourself: Is this 100% true? What's the evidence *for* and *against* this belief? Whose voice is this really?

- **Choose a new truth.** Replace the belief with one that empowers you. Example: *"I'm not qualified"* becomes *"I'm* *constantly learning and growing, and that makes me powerful."*

- **Speak it daily.** Your words shape your world. I began creating affirmations to interrupt negative thoughts and reinforce the truth I wanted to live in.

- **Celebrate the wins.** Every time you do something courageous, no matter how small—acknowledge it. Confidence is built through consistency,

Even after years of experience, I still remember the first time I was invited to speak at a major conference. Instead of excitement, I felt panic. *Why me? What if they realize I don't belong here?* I almost turned it down. But then I thought about all the people I've helped, all the experience I've gained, and I reminded myself: I do belong here. That moment changed everything. I stood on that stage, owned my story, and walked away realizing that imposter syndrome was nothing more than a liar in my head. Today I celebrate that I have been on over 25 stages speaking, sharing my stories or facilitating leadership development workshops in the last 2 years of making this leap.

Final Thoughts

Self-doubt may visit, but it doesn't get to stay. You are not behind. You are worthy of every room you step into, every dream you pursue, and every success that's calling your name. Your confidence isn't something you find. It's something you reclaim and you're already on your way.

Action Steps: Break Free and Own It

- **Call Fear Out.**
  Don't let it hide. Write down exactly what fear is whispering to you. Be honest—because what you don't name, you can't tame.

- **Check Your Inner Critic.**
  That voice saying, "You're not qualified" or "Who do you think you are?"—yeah, that one. Flip the script. Write a bold truth next to every lie and speak it out loud like you mean it.

- **Document the Wins—Even the Small Ones.**
  Confidence grows with evidence. Did you show up today? Speak up in a meeting? Send the email you were scared to write? Write it down. Stack your wins.

- **Create a "Brag File."**
  This isn't about ego—it's about remembering who you are. Save every compliment, client win, testimonial, or reminder of the difference you've made. Refer back to it every time imposter syndrome creeps in.

- **Practice Your Power Statement.**
  Say it with your chest. "I'm [your name], and I help [your people] get [your result] through [your method]." Speak it like the expert you are. Because you are.

- **Do the Scary Thing Anyway.**
  That thing you've been putting off because fear is loud? Do it. The clarity and confidence you want is on the other side of that action. Pick one thing and commit this week.

- **Visualize the Win.**
  Take 5 minutes to see yourself showing up bold—on stage, in the room, making the offer. Feel it. Believe it. Then go be her (or him, or them).

Bonus - 5 Powerful Statements to Silence the Inner Critic

- " I belong here. I am qualified, prepared, and chosen for this moment."

- "Perfection isn't required for impact. I'm growing and capable, right now."

- "My voice matters, and I refuse to shrink to make others comfortable."

- "Fear is just a feeling. I can still move forward with courage."
- "I don't need to know everything to be worthy. What I know is enough."

Instructions

1. Pick any of the 5 powerful statements above that speak directly to what resonates best with you and speak them in the mirror, write them down, or record them in your voice. Say it daily to train the subconscious mind so you start believing it.
2. Identify 3 limiting beliefs you've been carrying. Write down where they came from.
3. For each one, write a new empowering belief to replace it.
4. Celebrate one thing you did this week that challenged your doubt. You deserve and have the right to celebrate you!

Chapter 3:
Choosing to Reinvent Yourself

Now that you realize it's your time to be convicted to growing and to truly rebuild the confidence you once had, I want to share what helped me start reinventing my own life. First, I made the decision to grow, even without knowing exactly how or what was next. I committed to a daily journey of growth, understanding that each step forward was progress. My next move had to be my best move, and I embraced learning and growing as I went.

Next, I had to detach myself from the identity tied to my past. Often, we seek validation in titles or from others' expectations, but people-pleasing can be the biggest hindrance to growth. Letting go of that need for external validation and those old definitions of success opened the door to truly stepping into my purpose and embracing my authentic self.

It's okay to unlearn and relearn. In fact, it's essential. During my transition out of corporate life and through extreme burnout, I realized that speaking up and seeking help could have made a difference. I had worn the "Superwoman" cape, believing asking for help was a sign of weakness, which led to long hours and eventual burnout. But there are no regrets—every step led me to where I am now, writing this book and living my purpose.

Releasing the old version of myself and being open to renewal, reinvention, and learning new things about who I am has been transformative. It's about looking in the mirror and saying, "You've got this," and being intentional about reinventing your life.

There comes a moment—often quiet, but deeply transformative— when you realize that staying where you are is no longer an option. You may not know what the future holds, but something inside of you whispers, *"This can't be it."* That moment, as subtle or loud as it may be, is the beginning of your rise.

For me, that moment came after months of emotional exhaustion. I had already made the difficult decision to step away from a career that no longer served me, and I was still grieving the unexpected loss of my partner. I remember sitting in my car after yet another day of crying in silence, and whispering to myself, *"You can't stay here."* Not just physically—but mentally, spiritually, emotionally. I had survived, yes. But I wasn't living on purpose. And I knew I couldn't keep shrinking to fit into spaces that no longer aligned with who I was becoming.

The decision to reinvent your life doesn't happen overnight. It's a choice you make daily. It's waking up and saying, "I'm going to show up today—even if I'm scared. Even if I don't have it all figured out."

At first, I was paralyzed by fear. I didn't have a plan. I didn't know how I was going to make money. I just knew that I couldn't keep living a life that didn't feel aligned. I gave myself permission to start small. I dusted off old journals and wrote out my plan, my dreams, and my ideas for the future. I listened to motivational podcasts and read self help books. I got still long enough to hear my own voice again—the one I had ignored for years while chasing success that didn't fulfill me.

What Reinvention Actually Looks Like

Reinvention isn't about pretending the past didn't happen. It's about choosing to rise in spite of it. It's acknowledging the setback and using it as fuel. It's recognizing that the power to pivot exists within you—even when your circumstances try to convince you otherwise.

Reinvention is not a single decision; it's a series of decisions:

- Choosing to believe that your story isn't over.

- Choosing to let go of the version of yourself that only knew how to survive.

- Choosing to see possibilities where there once was only a setback.

- Choosing to move forward even when the road isn't clear ahead.

One of the most powerful things I did was start writing again. Journaling. Speaking. Coaching myself through my own uncertainty. It wasn't perfect, but it was forward. I stopped waiting for the right time or the perfect plan—and started trusting the process.

I started saying "yes" to opportunities that felt scary but aligned. My first speaking gig after leaving my career wasn't glamorous—it was in a small room with 25 people—but I showed up like it was a stadium. That day, something in me reawakened. I realized that I didn't have to wait to be chosen—I could choose myself.

One of the steps I encourage you to take is to ask yourself, "*What kind of life do I want to create moving forward? "What does my going-forward plan look like?" What vision do I have for myself?"* When you start defining that vision, you're essentially creating a blueprint for your future. One of the things I did was create a new vision board. I wrote down affirmations and clearly articulated my vision—not just cutting out pictures, but writing it all out and making it plain, as the scripture says. I mapped out what success looks like for me—not what others expected, but what I truly wanted.

Taking small, aligned actions was key. Confidence isn't something you wake up with—it's something you build with small, intentional steps. The thing about confidence is that it's like a muscle—it takes repetition. The more you work on the areas where you feel less confident, the more you build it over time. Consistency and intentionality turn those small steps into big leaps.

Each act of courage—like when I created my first workshop, recorded my podcast, or spoke on stages for corporations and organizations—

built that muscle. Hearing feedback from people who resonated with my story and found value in my message fueled my confidence even more. It wasn't about seeking validation but about realizing the impact I was making. That impact became my biggest inspiration and motivation to keep going.

It's also crucial to surround yourself with people and environments that match the level you're aiming for. One of the things that truly helped me during my season of setbacks, when I was figuring out my next move, was joining communities. I remember attending the Next Level Speakers Conference in June 2023. I went because one of my mentors and inspirations, Dr. Eric Thomas, also known as ET the Hip-Hop Preacher, was one of the speakers. I had invested in one of his programs, the Game Changers Speakers Program, back in 2020 to become a certified motivational speaker. But despite the investment, I hadn't moved the needle due to life's challenges.

In 2023, seeing him pop up on my social media feed reignited my determination, and I knew I had to attend that event. I went to Georgia, and the experience was transformative. Dr. Thomas's words struck a chord: *"Some of you don't need another mastermind, another conference, or another personal development course. You just need to move the needle."*

That was my conviction moment. At that point, I hadn't launched my podcast or fully developed my brand because I was caught up in perfectionism. But his words reminded me that action was more important than perfect conditions. When I returned to Maryland, I committed to applying the insights from that conference. I focused on creating content, promoting myself as a motivational speaker, coach, and workshop facilitator, and making an impact in every room I stepped into. I knew my gifts and purpose were bigger than my zip code.

That's why I can't stress enough the importance of aligning yourself with people who are on the same journey. Meeting new people can be intimidating—joining a new community, attending a networking event, or stepping into a focus group can bring about anxiety and the fear of not knowing what to say or how to engage. Much of that stems from a lack of confidence. It's natural to feel hesitant about talking to someone new or putting yourself out there. But remember, it's about taking baby steps.

Not all communities or events are in person; virtual networking can be just as powerful. You'd be surprised how many people are out there looking for a community or others with similar interests. Whatever you're passionate about, there's a community for you.

For me, stepping into entrepreneurship meant embracing my calling as a speaker. I knew motivational speaking, confidence coaching, and business strategy were among my top gifts. To nurture that, I joined a community of like-minded speakers who motivated, encouraged, and empowered me to keep learning and growing.

The same applied to starting the Convicted to Grow Podcast. I attended a conference on podcast monetization and growth, where I met other podcasters and learned to be confident in my podcasting journey. You're not on this journey alone. Many others face the same imposter syndrome, fear, and doubt, and they're looking to connect, too.

I challenge you to be the change agent. Just as I transformed my challenges into opportunities and became more confident in my speaking and coaching, you can do the same. I recently hosted a 21-day Women's Confidence Challenge, and I saw firsthand how many others are striving to grow in their confidence and show up boldly and authentically in their lives, careers, and businesses.

Your Next Level Is a Choice

We often wait for permission—to lead, to start, to dream again. But here's the truth: no one's coming to save you. The decision to elevate is yours.

If you're reading this, I want you to know: the same power that helped me choose again is already inside you. You don't need to know every step. You just need to decide that staying stuck is no longer your story.

You may be tired. You may be afraid. You may even feel unqualified for the vision that's in your heart—but I promise you, none of that disqualifies you from starting. You are allowed to grow. You are allowed to evolve. You are allowed to want more.

This chapter in your life might be hard—but it can also be the most defining one. When you decide to reinvent and elevate, you don't just change your direction—you change your identity. You become the version of yourself that no longer plays small. You begin to move from survival to significance.

I am living proof that you can rebuild after loss. You can start over after burnout. You can walk away from what's no longer aligned and still rise. And you don't have to do it perfectly—you just have to do it.

Final Thoughts

Reinventing yourself isn't about erasing who you were—it's about honoring your journey and choosing to evolve. Growth doesn't mean abandoning your past; it means learning from it, healing through it, and building something greater because of it. The power to begin again is already within you. Every setback, every challenge, every loss has been preparing you for this exact moment.

You are not defined by what happened to you—You are defined by how you choose to rise from it.

Action Steps : It's Time to Reinvent

As you close this chapter, remember that reinvention is a continuous journey. Here are some action steps to guide you forward:

- **Make the Choice.**
  Reinvention doesn't happen by accident—it's a decision. Declare it. Write this down:
  "I'm choosing to reinvent my life with clarity, confidence, and conviction."

Say it out loud. Mean it. It's not about waiting for permission—it's about claiming your next chapter.

- **Let Go of the Old Labels.**
  What titles, roles, or identities are keeping you boxed in? That includes labels like "people pleaser," "overthinker," or "always the strong one." Let them go—you don't need to carry who you *used* to be into who you're becoming.
  Write down the ones that no longer fit—and release them. You don't have to stay attached to what no longer serves you.

- **Get Clear on Who You're Becoming.**
  Ask yourself: Who do I want to be? How do I want to feel? What impact do I want to make?
  Don't overthink it—vision comes from clarity, not perfection. Visualize that version of you walking into a room. Confident. Clear. Aligned. Now start showing up as them.

- **Audit and Upgrade Your Environment.**
  Check your circle. Your habits. Your social feed. Are they aligned with where you're headed? If not, adjust. Reinvention requires you to surround yourself with what supports your growth—not your comfort zone.

- **Create a New Daily Standard.**
  Reinvention happens in your routines. Choose *one* habit this week that aligns with your reinvention—whether it's journaling, showing up on video, exercising, waking up earlier, or setting boundaries. Do it consistently.

- **Write to the Future You.**
  Take 5 minutes to write a letter to the version of you that's already living the life you're working toward. Thank them for not quitting. For rising. For becoming. This is your reminder that transformation is already happening—day by day.

- **Own the Process.**
  Reinvention isn't about perfection—it's about progress. Show yourself grace, but hold yourself accountable. You are not who you were. And that's a good thing.

Reinvention is your birthright. Rise, evolve, and live fully—not in spite of what happened to you, but because you chose to grow through it.

Part II:
The Rebuild

Chapter 4:
Rebuilding Confidence from the Ground Up

Once you've made the decision to reinvent and elevate your life, the real work begins. Reinvention doesn't happen without rebuilding—and the first brick you must lay is confidence. Not the surface-level, fake-it-til-you-make-it kind, but the type of confidence rooted in self-belief, clarity, and action. Confidence is the core foundation that everything else—your growth, your business, your leadership, your impact—is built upon.

I had to rebuild my confidence after grappling with grief, burnout, and the leap from corporate life into entrepreneurship. I didn't have a detailed plan, but I held onto the belief that I was meant for more. That belief was my anchor. Confidence didn't come from external applause or validation; it came from showing up every day, doing the work, and proving to myself that I could trust me again.

What I learned is that the rebuilding season isn't always pretty. There are days of uncertainty, discomfort, and questioning your why. You might feel emotional, anxious, or even have moments of depression. My rebuilding season wasn't pretty at first, but that's the nature of rebuilding—starting again when no one else is watching, deciding you're done being stuck, and saying no to things that no longer align with who you're becoming.

It means holding yourself accountable to your goals and believing you have no other choice but to pursue them. It means taking imperfect action even when you're scared and building consistency even when no one is clapping. Often, we look for validation or cheers from others, but what do you do when there's no one around? You become your own cheerleader, your own coach, and advocate for yourself. That's how I navigated my rebuilding phase.

They say confidence is like a muscle—it has to be built over time. You're not born with it; it's not something you just have from the start. Confidence develops even in childhood, with parents mentoring and instilling the belief that you can achieve something. That confidence comes from within. Even in adulthood, confidence needs to be nurtured and grown.

Think about going to the gym. You want a toned body, and you know it takes consistent reps and effort to get there. You have to put in the work regularly to see progress. Confidence is the same way. It's built through small steps, consistent exercises, and intentional actions, especially after a setback. There will be days that aren't easy, and times when you feel uncomfortable because you're stretching out of your comfort zone. But that's exactly where confidence grows—by doing it over and over again.

Remember the story of the Little Engine That Could, repeating "I think I can" as it climbed the hill. That simple phrase trained its subconscious mind to believe in its capability, until it shifted from "I think I can" to "I know I can."

Let this be a reminder: building confidence requires consistent effort, but it starts with small, intentional steps that you're capable of. I promise you, it's worth it.

The Myths About Confidence

One thing I want to clear up about confidence is the myths surrounding it. People often mistake confidence for arrogance, but that's not true. Confidence is grounded self-assurance, not an inflated ego. It doesn't mean you never doubt yourself; it means you move forward despite the doubt. Confidence is about pushing past the fear and uncertainty because your vision and purpose are bigger than your current reality.

Confidence isn't a personality trait; it's a skill you strengthen with practice. The more you put in the reps, the more resilient and capable you become, facing challenges with a steady sense of self. It's about standing tall in the face of obstacles without shrinking back into self-doubt.

Many myths about confidence can hold you back. As Coach Prime, Deion Sanders, says, "Don't let my confidence offend your insecurity." People might think you're "doing too much" or being extra, but they don't know your journey. They haven't seen the sleepless nights, the prayers, the hard work behind the scenes.

Confidence and willpower mean standing firm against the opinions of others and walking in your purpose boldly and confidently as the person you are meant to be. Confidence isn't something you wait to feel—it's something you build with every aligned decision you make. When you're rebuilding, don't look for perfection. Look for progress.

The Emotional Journey of Reinvention: It's Okay to Start Over

Rebuilding confidence was one of the most important chapters of my life—a journey that required deep internal work, self-reflection, and the courage to start over. I had been in consulting for over 20 years, specializing in recruiting and talent acquisition, building a successful career with my partner. But when grief and burnout hit after his passing, everything changed. I knew deep within that life had more for me than the path I had been on.

Stepping away from a well-established career to pursue my purpose was daunting. But I took a leap of faith, choosing to align my life with coaching and speaking—my true calling. Convicted to Grow Coaching was born from this shift.

It wasn't easy. Launching a new brand from scratch meant leaving behind my previous consulting business. While I could've continued, my heart wasn't in it anymore. This was a pivotal moment—a turning point where I realized it was okay to pivot, to start over, and to embrace a new direction.

The emotional journey of reinvention isn't linear or glamorous. It's about showing up even when your voice shakes, even when self-doubt tries to take over. I remember the first time I introduced myself as a speaker and coach after leaving my 9-5—my voice wavered, and I didn't fully believe it. But I kept saying: "I am a paid motivational speaker." I had to affirm my worth, even before I felt it. Slowly, with each affirmation, I trained my subconscious mind to align with the truth of my potential. Now, I walk into every room with the confidence of a six-figure speaker, always believing that my next milestone is just around the corner. Emphasis on paid, because I knew that if this was to become my new livelihood, I had to put it out into the universe with intention. I was no longer just sharing my story in churches or as a testimonial; this was now my bread and butter.

The more I affirmed it, the more I trained my subconscious mind to believe it. I walked into every room with the conviction of a successful, six-figure speaker on her way to seven figures. To this day, I say, "I am a multi-millionaire; time just hasn't caught up with me yet." Speaking things into existence is crucial. You have to walk in it before it feels natural.

As your confidence coach, I want you to remember this: confidence transforms your life, career, and business. When you're confident, you speak with conviction and clarity. You embrace opportunities instead of shrinking back. Too often, especially with the women I coach, we tend to dim our light. But when you know the value you bring to the table, you shine brightly.

Confidence also means raising your standards in business, relationships, and self-respect. When you walk into a room with that aura of confidence, people remember your presence and energy. You stop waiting for permission and start creating your own path. Building my own table with the Convicted to Grow brand was one of those bold moves that came from believing in myself and setting my own standards.

Starting over can feel like stepping into the unknown, but the truth is, we're all constantly reinventing ourselves. Whether it's your career, your business, or your mindset—each small decision you make leads to the next chapter of your life.

What I learned is that confidence is built in private long before it's publicly recognized. It's about the mindset work, the internal conversations, and the brave decisions made when no one is watching. When you align with your purpose, trust the process, and stay committed to the journey, the momentum builds.

Confidence is not just a trait—it's a skill that is developed over time through consistent actions. I always remind my clients: "Growth over perfection." It's not about waiting for everything to be perfect before you move forward. It's about showing up, doing the work, and taking those small, consistent steps.

So, if something in your life feels off, if you're restless or frustrated, it's okay to hit reset and pivot. If something in your life is pulling at you, causing sleepless nights or frustration, take a moment of stillness to reflect.. Meditate, pray, and reflect on what your next move should be. Silence the noise and unwanted distractions so you can get clear on your next chapter. Find clarity on where you're headed. With clarity, you'll stop second-guessing yourself and begin to trust the process.

In your journey of rebuilding, you might face days when it feels like nothing is happening. But trust me, every small win matters. Celebrate every step forward, no matter how small. Each one reinforces your belief in your own resilience and capability.

You can rebuild, even if you don't have all the answers. Trust yourself to take the next step. "

Repeat this affirmation daily: "I trust myself to rebuild, even if I don't have all the answers."

Growth over perfection is the mantra. Taking small steps, even when they're not perfect, builds your confidence over time.

Key Takeaways:

- It's okay to start over. Reinvention often requires bold steps toward change.

- Confidence is built through small, consistent actions—not perfection.

- Trust the process, and celebrate every small win along the way.

- Align with your purpose, and the right people, opportunities, and success will follow.

Action Steps for Rebuilding Confidence:

1. **Reflect on Your Current Confidence Level:**
   - Take a moment to assess where you stand in terms of confidence in different areas of your life (personal, career, business, relationships). Write down how you feel in each area and where you'd like to grow.

2. **Identify One Area to Focus On:**
   - Choose one area in your life where you need to rebuild or strengthen your confidence (e.g., public speaking, making decisions, networking). Start with one thing, and build from there.

3. **Set a Small, Achievable Goal:**
   - It could be something simple like speaking up in a meeting, making a connection with someone in your field, or posting your first video on social media. The key is to take action.

4. **Commit to Consistent Action:**
   - Break your goal into smaller, actionable steps and commit to taking one small step every day. Remember, consistency is more important than perfection. Even small progress adds up over time.

5. **Celebrate Every Win:**
   o At the end of each week, reflect on your progress. Celebrate every win—big or small. Writing down your achievements helps reinforce your confidence and motivates you to keep moving forward.

6. **Practice Self-Affirmations:**
   o Start your day with affirmations that align with your confidence-building journey. For example: "I trust myself to make confident decisions." "I am capable and worthy of success." Write them down and say them out loud.

7. **Track Your Progress:**
   o Keep a journal where you track your actions and thoughts around confidence. Notice patterns: what helps you feel more confident and what causes self-doubt? Use this journal to reflect and adjust your strategies as needed.

8. **Surround Yourself with Positive Influences:**
   o Identify people, groups, or communities that uplift and inspire you. Engage with them regularly to stay motivated and reinforce your belief in yourself. The right support system will help you stay on track.

9. **Embrace Imperfection:**
   o Don't wait for the "perfect" moment to take action. Embrace the idea that progress over perfection is what will help you grow. Commit to doing something imperfectly but consistently.

10. **Visualize Your Success:**
   o Spend a few minutes each day visualizing yourself achieving your goal. See yourself confident, successful, and thriving. Visualization strengthens your belief and aligns your mindset with the success you're working toward.

Chapter 5:
Letting Go of Who You Had to Be

There's a version of you that helped you survive, but that version can't come with you to where you're headed next. This truth hit me hard when I walked away from a career that no longer aligned with my purpose but to only cause me severe burnout. Months later, I was not only grieving the loss of a loved one but also the loss of a version of myself that I had outgrown. Transitioning to the next level of greatness means being prepared to outgrow certain things—whether it's friends, habits, or environments. My purpose became bigger than my zip code, and I realized taking bold moves were necessary for my next chapter of life.

Becoming a better you can be one of the most difficult yet freeing experiences. We don't just wake up confident; we peel back layers, unlearn old patterns, and unravel the truth that the person we had to be was strong, but not the whole story. Often, we conform to what others expect us to be, but it's crucial not to let people define us by past versions of ourselves. Each stage of life requires a different version of you, and it's okay to evolve and change.

Letting go of who you used to be is necessary because that version isn't equipped for where you're going. Your future is bright, and embracing growth means stepping out of familiar comfort zones to prepare for the incredible journey ahead.

The Survival Identity

Growing up, I was the dependable one. The overachiever. The one who made things happen and made people proud. I learned early on that strength equaled silence. That showing emotion might be seen as weakness. That productivity equaled value.

I carried that into adulthood—into my career, my relationships, my goals. I mastered the art of keeping it all together, even when I was falling apart inside. I was praised for being strong, but the truth was: I was tired of performing.

When I finally admitted that I needed a change, it felt like betrayal. Not just to others, but to the version of me who had worked so hard to build the life I had.

But here's what I learned: strength isn't holding it all together. Strength is knowing when it's time to let go.

No one prepares you for the grief that comes with growth. You expect to grieve relationships, jobs, or circumstances—but what about the version of you that had to survive it all?

I remember journaling one morning, tears streaming down my face, writing the words: *"I don't know who I am without the hustle."* I didn't just miss the job I left—I missed the person who found her identity in being needed, in being busy, in being strong.

But that version of me wasn't sustainable. She was exhausted, unfulfilled, and slowly breaking.

Letting go meant grieving her—and then choosing to release her with gratitude. She did her job. She got me through the storm. But she couldn't lead me into the next season.

Letting Go Is a Process

Letting go is a process. It's not an overnight decision, but a gradual peeling away of the old version of you—the identities you carried and the roles you felt responsible for. It's about acknowledging that the version of you who helped you survive may not be the one who can take you to where you're headed next.

Asking the Hard Questions

To truly let go, you must ask yourself some hard questions:

- Who did I become in my current life to be accepted by others?
- What did I sacrifice to be accepted?
- What version of me is no longer serving my future?

These questions aren't surface-level; they're soul-deep. They guide you to the freedom you didn't know you needed. Just like I had to grieve not only the loss of a loved one but also the old version of myself, you, too, can release who you had to be and step into who you are becoming.

Embracing the Transition

Transitions are never easy. Whether it's outgrowing friends, habits, or environments, each step away from the familiar is a step toward growth. It's recognizing that your purpose is bigger than your zip code, and that sometimes outgrowing what's comfortable is the only way to step into what's next.

Choosing to Release with Gratitude

Letting go isn't just about shedding the past; it's about releasing it with gratitude. The old version of you was strong, but that wasn't the whole story. It served its purpose. Now, you choose to lead with clarity and confidence. You choose to pivot into a new season, even when it's challenging. Embrace this new season to rise stronger. Step confidently into the new phase of your life, knowing that growth often requires leaving the familiar behind.

The Moment I Chose Me

For the first time, I chose "ME". Not the version of me that looked good on paper. Not the one who made everyone else comfortable. But the version of me who wanted peace, alignment, and purpose. The moment I chose myself was the moment I turned away from playing it safe. I had the opportunity to return to a familiar environment, a comfortable salary, and the old version of myself that had led to burnout. But saying yes to that would have meant abandoning the woman I was becoming. Even in my nine-to-five, I had no time to nurture my passion or my purpose. My purpose was my voice—speaking, coaching, helping others to build confidence and resilience. How could I serve the masses if I remained anchored to a job that drained me?

I'm not suggesting that everyone should quit their job on a whim. In today's world, with rising costs and economic uncertainty, having a plan is crucial. But for me, taking that leap years ago was necessary. It was a risk, but one I had to take because I believed in myself.

When you trust the process and take that leap of faith, it can yield abundance and success. Back then, there was no plan B for me—it had to work. Today, I'd advise you to have a plan, but never lose sight of that faith in yourself. Trust that every move you make, even the uncertain ones, can lead to growth and greatness.

Who Are You Without the Pressure?

That's the question that broke me open in the best way. Who am I without the need to prove, produce, or perform? If I'm not the strong one, am I still valuable? If I'm not hustling, am I still worthy? The answer, of course, is yes. You are worthy even in stillness, even in softness, even when you're not fixing everything for everyone. Your worth isn't tied to an action or someone else's measure. You are worthy because you are here, with the knowledge, skills, and ability to produce.

Letting go of who you had to be is about giving yourself permission to be whole. I challenge you today: give yourself permission to succeed, to try something new, to make yourself a priority, to believe in yourself. You don't need validation or a green light from anyone else. Once you let go of that, you become whole, truly valuable, and worthy.

The power of becoming is immense. Once I released the old version of myself, something beautiful began to happen. I stopped apologizing for taking up space, started honoring my boundaries, and gave myself permission to be seen without the armor. For the first time in a long time, I felt free—not because life got easier, but because I got more honest with myself. Rebuilding confidence after a setback isn't just about doing more; it's about becoming more of who you really are. And the truth is, you are becoming and evolving into that confident individual you were always meant to be.

The Power of Becoming -Reflection Questions

1. What version of you are you still holding onto out of fear or familiarity?
2. What beliefs have you carried that are no longer true?
3. What would it look like to show up as your most authentic self today?

Affirmations for Release

These affirmations aren't just feel-good statements—they're mindset shifts. They're permission slips. They are daily reminders to speak over yourself about what you may have been waiting to hear from others.

I want you to do more than just read these. I want you to *declare* them. Speak them out loud. Write them in your journal.Stick them on your mirror. Record them on your phone and play them back to yourself when self-doubt tries to creep in. Because here's the truth: your words have power and the more you affirm the version of you that's rising, the more confident, aligned, and free you'll become.

- I release the need to perform to be validated by others.
- I am allowed to evolve and outgrow what no longer fits.
- I honor who I was, but I'm choosing who I'm becoming.
- I am no longer shrinking to make others comfortable.

Say these daily. Say them until they feel real. Because your rebuilding isn't about perfection—it's about giving yourself permission to rise above to your next chapter of greatness.

Final Thoughts

Letting go of who you had to be isn't the end of your story—it's the beginning of a bold, new chapter. It's your invitation to be real, to be whole, and to rise with confidence. No more second-guessing. No more shrinking. No more trying to fit into a version of yourself that was only meant for survival. Now is the time to show up fully, freely, and unapologetically. You are special. You are needed. And if no one's told you lately—you are amazing. You are enough. You don't have to prove your worth. You don't have to have it all figured out. You just have to be willing to grow. You are allowed to change. You are allowed to evolve. And you are absolutely allowed to become the strongest, truest version of yourself. This is your permission to rise. You're not just rebuilding—you're becoming. And you were never meant to stay stuck. You were *Convicted to Grow*.

Action Steps

As you move forward, here are some actionable steps to help you continue this journey:

1. **Identify What No Longer Serves You**: Make a list of habits, roles, and mindsets that no longer align with your future self. Acknowledge their role in your journey, then consciously release them.

2. **Create a New Vision Board**: Visualize the person you're becoming. Include your aspirations, values, and the life you want to live. Let this vision guide your daily decisions.

3. **Practice Self-Compassion**: Be gentle with yourself as you navigate change. Reinvention is a process, and it's okay to take it one step at a time.

4. **Set Boundaries**: Protect your energy and time by setting boundaries that align with your new direction. Say no to what no longer fits, and yes to what propels you forward.

5. **Celebrate Your Progress**: Acknowledge and celebrate every step you take towards becoming your true self. Each milestone is a testament to your growth.

Chapter 6:
Rediscovering Your Why

There's a moment in every rebuilding season when you pause and ask yourself, "What is my why? Why am I even doing this? Why am I starting over? Why am I choosing the hard route instead of the familiar one? Why does any of this matter? Why me?" Those questions aren't signs of weakness; they're signs of awakening. When everything around you has changed, when your titles no longer fit, when you've outgrown people, and your past feels unfamiliar, it's your why that keeps you grounded. I often ask my clients this very question, and their answers vary—some say their kids, some say giving back to the community or retiring their parents.. Whatever your why is, it's the anchor that drives you to press forward, to rebuild, and to rise stronger. Your why is the connecting point to your journey of rebuilding and rising.

Rediscovering your why isn't just a journey—it's a homecoming. It's that pivotal moment when you peel back the layers of expectation and noise to reconnect with the core of who you are and what sets your soul on fire. It's that quiet but powerful realization that your purpose never left you—it was simply waiting for you to come back. And when you do, you step forward with a confidence that's unshakable, because it's rooted in the very essence of who you are and what you're meant to bring into the world.

Rediscovering your why is essential to rebuilding your confidence because it reconnects you to what matters most. When you've experienced a setback—whether in life, career, or identity—it's easy to feel unanchored and uncertain. But purpose is what grounds you. It reminds you that you're not starting over—you're starting from experience, with deeper clarity and stronger intention. Your why becomes the internal compass that silences self-doubt, fuels resilience, and gives your next steps meaning. Confidence doesn't come from knowing exactly how everything will unfold—it comes from knowing why you're showing up in the first place.

Losing Your Why in the Fire

What do you do when you lose your why in the fire? When you no longer feel anchored after a setback? When I walked away from my successful corporate career, I had no why. I was burnt out, drained, and uninspired. And then, a few months later, after losing my partner, I lost even more. I didn't just lose people and titles; I lost clarity. For a while, I was moving but not anchored, just going with the flow. I was good at a lot of things, with decades of experience in recruiting, HR, and leadership. But just because you're good at something doesn't mean it's your purpose. I was building a life that looked good on paper but left me empty inside. It wasn't until I got really, really quiet that I realized I had been chasing a version of success that no longer served me. I had outgrown it, and I had to redefine what success and purpose looked like going forward. Often, setbacks make you lose sight of the vision and the why because the focus shifts to the pain rather than the promise. But when you decide that giving up on your why is not an option, you find the fuel to keep fighting and moving forward, no matter what the current season looks like.

Losing our why often happens subtly, like a slow fade rather than a sudden disappearance. It can slip away in the daily grind, buried under endless to-do lists, societal expectations, and the relentless pursuit of external validation. When we face setbacks or experience burnout, our why can become overshadowed by survival mode, leaving us feeling disconnected and adrift. The ambitions and passions that once fueled us get lost in the noise of responsibilities and the expectations of others. But acknowledging that we've lost our why is the first step to reclaiming it, paving the way for a deeper, more meaningful rediscovery of purpose and passion.

The Importance of Purpose in the Rebuilding Phase

Rebuilding confidence without purpose is like constructing a house without a foundation—you'll always feel unstable. Your why is your anchor. It's what keeps you moving when you feel unseen, and what sustains you when you're tired, discouraged, or depleted.

That's why I always say: write the vision down and make it plain. . Create the vision board and visualize your success. . Put it where you can see it. Because when you forget why you started and feel weary in your well doing, your "why" along with your vision will remind you why you can't give up.

Purpose gives meaning to the mundane. It helps you endure the messy middle and resist the urge to give up when it gets heavy. When you're rooted in your why, every "no" becomes protection, not rejection. Setbacks become redirections. Delays become divine alignment.

Your why helps you guard your vision, protect your peace, and move forward with intention—not pressure.

And here's what I've learned from my own journey, and from coaching countless others: rediscovering your why isn't a one-time thing. It's a rhythm. A check-in. A conversation between your soul and your future. Life will shift. You will evolve. And your purpose might, too—and that's okay.

The key is staying open. Let every transition refine your why. Whether it's a career shift, a new business endeavor, a personal loss, or a major life transition, your why can be the compass that guides you through uncertainty and back to a place of confidence and clarity. Let every season reveal a little more of who you're called to be. Because your why isn't just about what you do—it's about who you are, who you're becoming, and the impact you're destined to leave behind.

The Day I Found My Why Again

The day I found my why again after my setback of burnout and grief actually happened on two occasions. The very first was in 2023. I remember waking up on a Saturday morning in a place of numbness; my grief hit me so hard that day. Grief can come and go, and that's why I always say never let anyone tell you when you should be healed—heal on your own accord. That particular morning, I woke up, prayed, and asked God, 'What does my next look like?' In that moment of meditation and stillness, I felt like an angel tapped me on the shoulder. I looked at my first book, 'I Found Strength in My Struggles,' written in 2017, and remembered the journey. I flipped to Chapter 7, titled 'Convicted to Grow,' and had a full-circle moment. Back then, I was trying to figure out my next steps amid life's struggles. I prayed and told God, 'If you allow me to see 45—just a few weeks away—I promise to be convicted of growing, changing, and becoming the best version of myself.' From that moment in May 2023, my Convicted to Grow movement began unfolding before my eyes. It's not just a title; it's a way of life, a movement, and a mantra I remember leading a workshop for a small group of women in transition. One woman—soft-spoken and unsure—shared how she hadn't spoken up for herself in years.

The second occasion I remember was when I was on TikTok Live. I would do these Monday Motivation Live sessions at noon—midday motivation on Mondays—every single Monday. I would give the audience 30 to 45 minutes of motivational, inspirational talk, really showing up for myself. During that time, not only was I putting in the reps as a speaker, but I was also rebuilding my confidence to put myself out there in front of people who didn't know me but followed me because they liked my content. It took courage to go live, and I did it consistently every single Monday.

I remember seeing the audience comments, people saying things like, 'Thank you, I needed to hear this.' One time, there was a guy who put in the chat, 'Coach Tressa, thank you so much for your inspirational content. You don't know how impactful your words are.. In fact, I was contemplating taking my life. I was in a place of depression, feeling like I no longer belonged here. I had even sent messages to my family and friends saying goodbye. The next morning, I knew that was going to be my last day. But when I opened my phone to close my apps, TikTok was still open, and the very first video I saw was you, Tressa, saying, 'I will not take an L in this season.' Your video changed my life. It made me realize that I, too, matter and that I have a purpose bigger than my current struggles. Thank you for saving my life.'

In that moment, not only did he say it publicly in the chat for others to see, but it gave me chills. It made me understand that I can't cheat on my gift. I can't cheat on my why—my purpose of motivating, encouraging, and inspiring through speaking, coaching, and workshops. That moment, in the latter part of 2023, still in my season of grief, was my fuel to say, 'Tressa, you can't give up because there are others who need your motivation, encouragement, guidance as a coach and you have a purpose to finish what you started.

Your WHY Is Tied To Your Purpose

Rediscovering my why wasn't a one-time event. It was a series of quiet moments, brave decisions, and honest conversations that led me back to my calling.

Here's what I want you to know: you don't need to have it all figured out to rediscover your purpose. You don't need a five-year plan, a perfect title, or anyone else's approval. What you need is curiosity, compassion, and the courage to explore. Start with where you are. What brings you peace, even in chaos? What have you always been drawn to but never gave yourself permission to pursue? When do you feel most like yourself? What have you overcome that someone else might need to hear about? These aren't just questions—they're keys. And if you give yourself the space to reflect and listen, you'll realize the clarity you've been searching for has been inside you all along. You don't have to be ready—you just have to be *willing* to start.

Your why is deeply tied to your purpose—it's the heartbeat of everything you're building. It's not just about what you do; it's about *why* you show up, even when it's hard. Your why reminds you that your voice matters, that your journey has meaning, and that the setbacks you've faced weren't in vain. Purpose isn't just about having a title or chasing success—it's about aligning with something bigger than yourself. Your why gives your purpose legs to stand on when the pressure gets heavy. It becomes your anchor when life tries to pull you off course. And when you're rooted in your why, you don't just rebuild—you rise, with clarity, with conviction, and with confidence that you were made for more.

Purpose Check-In: Realign with What Matters Most

Let's be real for a second—life gets loud. We pour into jobs, family, clients, content, and everything else, and before we know it... we're moving but not aligned. That's why I always say: check in with yourself. When you reconnect with your *why*, you begin to rebuild from a place of purpose—not pressure.

This isn't about having it all figured out. It's about getting honest, getting quiet, and remembering what truly fuels you.

Grab your notebook—the one you committed to at the start of this journey—and take a moment to reflect on these questions.

- When was the last time I felt fully alive doing what I love?
- Am I chasing goals that align with *me*, or goals that look good to others?
- What have I been tolerating that no longer fits where I'm going?
- Who or what am I called to impact with my story, my voice, and my gifts?
- Does how I show up daily reflect the future I say I want?

Take your time. Sit with these. There's no "right" answer—just your truth.

Because your *why* is connected to your *purpose*. And when you're aligned with that, you don't have to force it. You don't have to pretend. You just *become.*

This is your moment to get real with yourself and grow forward—because you're not just here to rebuild. You're here to rise.

Give Yourself Permission to Pivot

Sometimes we cling to an old "why" because it's what we've always known. It's familiar. It's safe. But growth demands honesty—and often, it demands a shift.

Here's what I want you to know: you have permission to pivot. You're allowed to evolve. You're allowed to change direction, to walk away from what no longer aligns, and to choose what fuels you instead of what drains you. Pivoting doesn't mean you failed. It means you're listening to your spirit. It means you've outgrown a space that once served you. That's not disloyalty—that's development.

You're not lost—you're evolving. And every bold pivot you make is preparing you for the purpose you didn't even know was waiting for you.

What inspired you five years ago may not move you today—and that's okay. What used to be your "why" might have shifted because you've shifted. That's not confusion—that's clarity rising.

This is your season to lean into that shift. Don't resist it. Honor it.

The Connection Between Confidence and Your Purpose

Let's get into it—your confidence and your purpose are connected. When you're unsure about why you're doing something, you'll question everything. You'll start shrinking in rooms you were built to shine in. You'll downplay your gifts. You'll hesitate to speak up. But when you're rooted in purpose? You move differently. You show up with intention. You walk into spaces with clarity, not comparison.

Confidence doesn't mean you have all the answers—it means you're aligned with something *real*. Something that pulls you forward when motivation fades. Your purpose reminds you that your voice matters. That your story carries weight. And that what you've been through wasn't random—it was preparation.

The more you reconnect with why you're here, the more boldly you'll show up. Not from ego, but from alignment. Not from pressure, but from peace. Because when you know your purpose, you don't have to perform—you just walk in it.

My Why, In This Season

In this season, my why is crystal clear: I'm here to help others rebuild their confidence, reclaim their voice, and rise after the fall—because I had to do it first. I know what it feels like to lose everything you thought defined you. To smile in public and cry in private. To be strong for everyone else while silently asking, *"What about me?"*

But I also know the power of choosing to start over. Of doing the inner work. Of rebuilding brick by brick, not just a brand—but a version of myself that's rooted in truth, not titles. I've learned that the calling doesn't stop just because the storm shows up. And that sometimes, the pain is what activates the purpose.

So my why in this season isn't about being seen—it's about being in alignment. It's about creating impact, not just content. It's about reminding people that they're not alone, that their story still matters, and that this setback won't be the end of them.

I show up because I'm convicted to grow and every time I pour into someone else, I rise too.

Final Thoughts

Rediscovering your why is not about having it all figured out—it's about getting reconnected to what makes your soul breathe again. It's about remembering that your life has meaning beyond the roles you've played or the setbacks you've survived. You're not too late, and you're not behind. The vision may have shifted, but the purpose is still there—waiting for you to answer it.

Let go of the pressure to have a perfect plan. What matters is that you're willing to explore, to get quiet, to ask the hard questions, and to listen to what rises. Because when you're rooted in your why, confidence hits differently.. It's not performance—it's presence. And from that place? You don't just rebuild. You rise with conviction.

Action Steps

1. **Write Your Why Statement**
   In your notebook, complete this sentence:
   "In this season, I show up because..."
   Let it be raw. Let it be real. This is your personal anchor.

2. **Create a Visual Reminder**
   Write your why on a sticky note, journal cover, or vision board. Put it somewhere you'll see every day. Your purpose deserves space in your daily environment.

3. **Do a Confidence Alignment Check**
   Reflect: Does how you're spending your time and energy reflect your current purpose? If not, where can you make a small shift this week?

4. **Speak Life Over Your Why**
   Say this out loud every morning this week:
   "I am aligned. I am evolving. And I am showing up for what I'm called to do."

5. **Share It With Someone You Trust**
   Tell a mentor, friend, or accountability partner what your rediscovered why is. Speaking it out loud makes it real—and powerful.

Journal Prompts:

- What did I love doing before the world told me who to be?
- When do I feel the most alive?

- Who am I when I'm not catering to others?
- What do I want to be remembered for?

Give yourself permission to sit with these. No pressure. No performance. Just truth.

Part III:
The Rise

Chapter 7:
Becoming Who You Were Always Meant to Be

There comes a point in your journey where you realize you're no longer the person you used to be. Not because everything is perfect, but because you've done the work. You've faced the pain, rewritten the story, embraced the healing, and reclaimed your voice. *This* is the rise.

The rise isn't about reaching a single destination—it's about stepping into your full, authentic self. It's about owning your story without shame and leading with courage. It's what happens when confidence, clarity, and commitment collide.

Becoming who you are always meant to be starts with a single, bold decision: to honor your true self. There's a version of you waiting on the other side of obedience, healing, and courage. You're not defined by your past; you're shaped by your rise. Many of us spend years people-pleasing, seeking validation, and fitting into molds that weren't designed for us. Along the way, we lose ourselves, muting our voices, dimming our light, and minimizing our dreams. But deep down, you've always known: there's more. There's someone inside you who wants to be seen—not the version you learned to perform, but the version you were born to embody.

I knew there was more to me than being a corporate leader. While my nine-to-five shaped my work ethic, integrity, and character, I realized I had an entrepreneurial spirit yearning to be unleashed. For years, I didn't take it seriously because I was flowing with what others expected of me. But after facing burnout and grief, I understood that life is too short not to try, not to pursue what sets your soul on fire.

Yes, it's scary and uncertain, but you have to be your biggest investment. Just like people buy lottery tickets hoping to win, you have to bet on yourself. Tell yourself that you are becoming who you were always meant to be, and step boldly into that destiny. Give yourself permission to be who you've been all along.

Why Becoming Is a Process

When you're evolving into a new version of yourself, it's not an overnight shift; it's a journey that takes time. For me, becoming who I am today was a process and still is a process. It meant going through therapy to heal from grief and depression, and putting in the work to rebuild my confidence. I also started making self care a priority to ensure my peace and energy was protected. I had to stop trying to revert to the old, comfortable version of myself that served a past season. Letting go of the illusion of going back and leaning into old habits or circles was crucial. The real transformation happens in the process, not the promise.

So many of us want the end goal but resist the journey. The process is where the most profound transformation takes place. That's why I always emphasize celebrating your small wins and embracing the process. Yes, it's messy and feels like an in-between space. You grieve who you used to be while still figuring out who you're becoming. But don't rush it; this is sacred ground.

The cost of holding on to an outdated version of yourself is comfort, but also confinement. Staying the same might feel safe, but it limits your growth, impact, and peace. Growth is a daily commitment. I had to shed past failures, grief, and anything that no longer aligned with who I was becoming. Through meditation, prayer, and therapy, I embraced the process. And while I'm still growing and evolving, I'm proud of the journey and the person I am today because I chose to embrace the process.

Ask yourself: What does it cost me to stay in this current version of myself?

- Does it cost you rest?
- Does it cost you alignment?
- Does it cost you your voice?
- Does it cost you opportunities that require the next version of you to say yes?

Every time you shrink, stay quiet, or second-guess your truth to keep others comfortable, you pay a price. But the good news is: you don't have to keep paying it.

You can choose to evolve and be convicted of growing.

Signs You're Evolving

Let me say this loud and clear: You're not broken—you're shifting and sometimes, that discomfort is actually growth. And that tension you feel right now? That restlessness? That discomfort? That's not failure—it's evolution in real time.

You're becoming the next version of yourself, and it doesn't always feel graceful or clear. In fact, most of the time, it feels like you're standing in the middle of what was and what's next—questioning everything. But don't mistake that uncertainty for being lost. You're not lost, love—you're *becoming*.

I remember going through this season myself. Right after I walked away from my corporate career and was still navigating the pain of loss, I started feeling completely out of alignment with everything that used to make sense. I wasn't excited about the work I once loved. I was showing up in spaces that felt draining instead of empowering. I looked around and realized... I didn't fit anymore. And truthfully, I wasn't meant to.

But I stayed for a while. Why? Because it was familiar. Because I didn't want to disappoint anyone. Because people expected me to be the strong one, the "put-together" one, the one who always had it figured out.

But here's what I learned: just because something's familiar doesn't mean it's right for your next level.

Here are some signs that you're becoming the next version of yourself:

- You're craving authenticity more than approval.
- You're uncomfortable in environments that used to feel familiar.
- You're dreaming bigger, but your current life feels too small.
- You're no longer willing to shrink to make others feel safe.
- You're starting to ask, "What do I want?" instead of "What do they expect?"

If you've felt this lately—you're not alone. And you're not lost. You're just becoming.

You're Not Behind—You're Building

Social media will have you thinking you're late. That everyone else has figured it out but you. But let me tell you this: **you're not behind. You're building.**

Becoming takes time. It requires intentionality, boundaries, and reflection. It requires releasing timelines and trusting the process. There's no rush to arrive—because every version of you along the way is sacred.

Stop measuring your pace by someone else's progress. Start asking yourself: Am I becoming more of who I really am?

If the answer is yes, you're right on time.

What It Means to Rise

To rise means you've decided not to be defined by your past, your pain, or your circumstances. It means you've taken the pieces of what was broken and built something stronger. Rising is resilience in motion. It's showing up boldly—not because life is easy, but because you're rooted in purpose.

For me, the rise began quietly. There was no grand announcement. Just a moment where I looked in the mirror and no longer saw a woman trying to survive. I saw a woman who had made it through. A woman who had been buried under grief, burnout, and fear—and who had chosen to grow anyway.

That moment didn't come overnight. It came after months of tears, therapy, prayer, reflection, and intentional action. I had to unlearn old habits. I had to choose self-worth over self-doubt. I had to reintroduce myself to the version of me that had been buried beneath roles, responsibilities, and other people's expectations.

There was a specific morning I remember vividly. I woke up, opened my journal, and instead of writing about what hurt, I wrote about what was possible. That simple act was symbolic—it meant I was no longer defined by pain, but driven by purpose. That was my turning point.

My Becoming Season

There was a season I had to completely redefine who I was outside of loss, outside of a career, outside of who people thought I should be. I was grieving, yes—but I was also awakening.I had been operating in a version of me that was strong, dependable, put-together and exhausted. I was leading everyone else but felt disconnected from myself. Becoming started with a whisper: "You don't have to stay here."

That whisper became a decision. That decision became a habit. That habit became a lifestyle. And that lifestyle became a brand, a mission, and a movement. But it didn't start on a stage. It started in stillness. In solitude. In surrender.

That's where your becoming begins too.

Final Thoughts

Becoming who you were always meant to be isn't about arriving—it's about aligning.You don't have to chase it. You just have to remove what's been blocking it.You've always had the gifts, the fire, and the voice. Now, it's about owning it without apology. No more waiting for permission. No more shrinking in spaces you've outgrown. You are not who you used to be—and that's a beautiful thing.

This season? It's about rising into the version of you that's been waiting on the other side of obedience, clarity, and conviction. Because the world doesn't need a version of you that just survives. It needs the version of you who shows up whole, confident, and aligned.

Action Steps

1. Write a Release Letter – Thank the old version of yourself who helped you survive. Honor her. Then, write what you're stepping into next.

2. Affirm Who You're Becoming – Speak this aloud: "I am becoming the person I prayed for. I release the past and rise with clarity, confidence, and peace."

3. Identify One Shift You're Ready to Make – What mindset, habit, or relationship needs to change to support the version of you that's rising?

You're not just rebuilding. You're becoming. And you were always Convicted to Grow.

Chapter 8:
Stepping Into Boldness

So here's the thing about stepping into boldness—let's just be honest. There comes a point in life when you're faced with a pivotal choice. You have to make a move, and sometimes that move has to be a bold one. It's easy and comfortable to play it safe, to stick to the familiar, and to stay within the lines. But when you decide to rise up and show up as the person you were truly created to be, that's when a bold step into something new becomes essential.

Boldness doesn't require you to have everything figured out. It shows up in the messy middle, in those seasons of setback, uncertainty, or stillness. It's that quiet yet persistent nudge telling you that fear doesn't get to have the final say. It's the realization that you already have the boldness within you, and you just need to activate it.

I knew I had to move forward when I was grappling with grief and burnout. I remember sitting in my house, feeling the weight of it all, and thinking, *I'm ready for a change.* Change is scary. It's uncertain, and it often feels like a huge risk. But I knew that if I wanted to step into my next level of greatness, my bold move required stepping out of my comfort zone—even if it meant relocating to a new state and starting over, turning a page to a brand-new chapter.

Sure, I could've stayed in my comfort zone and played it safe, but something deep within whispered, *This is your season. This is your time.* So I made a bold decision: even if I didn't have all the answers, I was going to try. I was going to stop hiding and start showing up.

And let me tell you, once you choose boldness, you never go back to being the same.

Boldness Isn't Loud—It's Liberating

Boldness isn't about being the loudest person in the room. It's not about having a spotlight, a big personality, or needing to prove anything to anybody. Boldness has *nothing* to do with volume—and everything to do with **value.**

Boldness is a **posture**—how you carry yourself when you walk into the room.

It's a **mindset**—how you choose to show up when fear tries to whisper in your ear.

It's a **decision**—a conscious choice to stop shrinking and start living fully.

Boldness is when you say:

> *"I'm not playing small anymore."*
> *"I'm done letting fear drive."*
> *"I'm showing up—even if my voice shakes."*

It's not about pretending you have it all together. It's about being willing to **move anyway**. It's about trusting your voice, your gift, and your growth—even when you're still figuring it out.

See, so many of us have buried parts of ourselves to stay likable, agreeable, or "professional."

We've dimmed our light to avoid making others uncomfortable.

We've silenced our brilliance to keep the peace.

And we've *waited*—for approval, for permission, for the perfect time.

Let me speak directly to that version of you: Boldness is not reserved for the confident—it's what creates confidence.Boldness is saying YES to the version of you that's been tucked away under layers of fear, comparison, self-doubt, and people-pleasing. It's saying:"I know there's more in me. And I'm ready to meet that version of myself."

Boldness doesn't ask, *"Will they accept me?"* It asks, *"Will I accept myself enough to show up, regardless?"*

So no—you don't need permission to rise. You don't need validation to speak. You don't need a title to take the lead.You just need a moment of courage to decide: this is the version of me I'm no longer hiding. That's boldness. That's liberation. And when you walk in it, you free others to do the same.

What's Been Holding You Back?

Let's pause for a real moment—not just to reflect, but to get radically honest. I want to ask you some questions that might rattle you a little. And that's okay. Growth starts when we're willing to look in the mirror and confront the truth of what's really been keeping us stuck.

Are you waiting until you feel "ready"?

Are you holding back because you think there's some magic moment coming—some future version of yourself that'll feel more confident, more prepared, more perfect?

I need you to hear this: *readiness is a decision, not a destination.* You don't become ready by waiting. You become ready by *moving.* So ask yourself: how many opportunities have you talked yourself out of because you were waiting on a feeling instead of trusting your calling?

Are you caught in the trap of comparison?

It's easy to scroll through social media, sit in meetings, or watch others thrive and think, *"They've got it all figured out and I'm still trying to get started."* But listen—just because you're in Chapter 1 doesn't mean you're not destined for greatness. Someone else's highlight reel should never make you feel behind in your own journey. Every step you take is a building block toward your own breakthrough. Your story is not a race—it's a revolution in the making.

Are you afraid of being seen, judged, or criticized?

Let's talk about that fear of visibility. I get it—putting yourself out there can feel vulnerable. Maybe you've been burned before. Maybe people have misunderstood you, underestimated you, or made you question your worth. But let me remind you of something powerful: when you hide your brilliance to avoid judgment, you rob the world of your impact. Playing small doesn't protect you—it keeps you stuck.

Here's the raw, unfiltered truth: you cannot be bold and blend in at the same time. Boldness demands that you step out. That you take up space. That you stand in the fullness of who you are—even if your hands shake and your voice quivers. Your next level? It lives beyond that fear. Your breakthrough doesn't come from perfection; it comes from your willingness to be unapologetically real.

It's time to get tired of shrinking. Tired of dimming your light. Tired of second-guessing your worth. Tired of watching life pass you by while you sit on the sidelines wondering, *"What if?"* The truth is, everything you want—the impact, the clarity, the confidence—is sitting on the other side of the fear you've been feeding.

So no more waiting for the perfect moment. No more comparing your lane to someone else's. No more hiding in the shadows, hoping not to be noticed. You were *born* to be noticed. Not for ego, but for *purpose.*

This is your wake-up call. Your invitation to rise and be bold. To embrace your quirks, your fears, your power, and your potential. To stop trying to fit in where you were never meant to blend. Because when you finally show up fully—as yourself, not someone else's version of success—that's when the shift happens. That's when doors open. That's when *everything changes.*

What will your breakthrough look like?

It begins with one bold decision: To stop hiding and start rising. To show up in all your imperfect, fierce, authentic glory. Because the world doesn't need a perfect version of you—it needs a present one.

What Stepping Into Boldness Looks Like

So what does boldness actually look like in real life? Let me break it down for you—because it's not always big and flashy. Sometimes, boldness is quiet but intentional. It's speaking up in the meeting, even when your heart is racing and your hands are sweating. It's sharing your story, even when you're not sure how it'll be received, because you know someone needs to hear it.

Boldness is raising your prices—and not flinching—because you finally believe you're worth it. It's launching the thing you've been sitting on, even if nobody claps yet, because you're no longer waiting for validation to move.

Boldness is not about waiting for a green light from someone else— it's about giving it to yourself. It's saying, *"I may be nervous, but I'm still showing up."* Because bold action isn't about the absence of fear. It's about the presence of purpose.

You Are the Bold One Been Waiting For

Boldness isn't reserved for the fearless—it's for the willing. The willingness to try. The willingness to show up. The willingness to grow in front of others while still figuring things out.

You don't have to wait until you feel 100% confident. Confidence is *built* in motion. And boldness? That's what sets it in motion. You've spent enough time playing small, questioning your worth, and dimming your light for fear of being "too much." But what if your *too much* is exactly what the world needs? What if your voice, your story, your presence is the breakthrough someone else has been praying for?

Boldness isn't about having it all figured out. It's about having the courage to move forward, even when the path isn't clear. It's the decision to show up when it would be easier to sit back. It's choosing progress over perfection, purpose over popularity, and growth over comfort. The truth is, most people don't lack ability—they lack boldness. But here's the good news: boldness is not something you wait for. It's something you activate.

You've already spent enough time second-guessing yourself. You've questioned your worth, overanalyzed your next move, and allowed fear to talk you out of opportunities that were *meant* for you. But what if the version of you you've been waiting on isn't "out there," in the future, somewhere far off? What if that version of you—the confident one, the one who leads, speaks up, makes impact, and walks with purpose—has been inside you all along, waiting for you to stop hiding?

You don't need to be louder or more polished. You don't need a bigger following, a perfect plan, or more validation. You just need to *trust yourself.* You just need to start saying yes to the real you—the version of yourself that knows you were created to lead, to serve, to build, and to shine.

This is your reminder: you were never waiting on permission. You were waiting on *alignment.* Boldness isn't something you step into once you're "ready"—it's the very thing that makes you ready. When you choose to be bold, you begin to unlock levels of clarity, strength, and confidence that have been sitting dormant, waiting on your decision to move.

So don't hold back anymore. Don't shrink to fit spaces that were never built for your full expression. Don't wait for the perfect moment, because the perfect moment is *now.* The bold version of you is not a dream—it's a decision. A daily one. A deliberate one.

Final Thoughts

Stepping into boldness is not about waiting until the fear disappears—it's about moving forward with it and choosing to grow anyway. Boldness doesn't demand perfection; it simply requires a decision.

You already have what it takes. The next level of your life is waiting on the real, confident, purpose-driven version of you to show up. So stand tall. Speak up. Take the step. Boldness is the doorway—and you're ready to walk through it.

And that decision starts with this:

- Today, I choose to show up.
- Today, I choose to lead.
- Today, I choose to grow—boldly, fearlessly, and unapologetically.

Action Steps: Activate Your Boldness

1. **Call Out the Fear**
   Write down one fear that has been keeping you stuck or silent. Then write a truth that counters it.
   Example: Fear – "I'm not qualified."
   Truth – "My experience, my voice, and my story are more than enough."

2. **Make One Bold Move This Week**
   Identify one area where you've been hesitating—then do the thing. Apply. Post. Pitch. Speak. Show up. Don't wait to be "ready"—act like it's already yours.

3. **Create a Boldness Affirmation**
   Speak this over yourself daily. Here's one to get you started:
   "I am bold. I don't shrink. I lead with confidence and move with purpose—even when it's uncomfortable."

4. **Rewrite Your Narrative**
   Choose one story you've been telling yourself that no longer serves you—something like, "I always play it safe" or "I'm not a speaker." Rewrite it boldly.
   "I take risks that align with my growth."
   "I use my voice with power and clarity."

5. Reflect and Record

Journal on this prompt:

"If I gave myself full permission to be bold this year, what would I do differently?"

Let your bold vision speak louder than your doubts.

Chapter 9:
Daily Habits That Build Unshakeable Confidence

Confidence isn't something you stumble upon—it's something you build, brick by brick, day by day. And if you've been waiting for a magical moment where you suddenly wake up confident, I'm here to lovingly shake that idea loose. Confidence is a muscle, and it grows with consistent use. You don't need more motivation. You need rhythm. You need practice. You need habits that align with who you're becoming. It's not reserved for a lucky few, and it doesn't suddenly show up on the days you feel good. Real, unshakeable confidence is built in the daily choices you make—especially when no one's watching.

It's easy to assume that some people were just born confident. But the truth? Confidence is a byproduct of commitment. It's created through intentional habits that reinforce your identity and remind you of your power. Whether you're rebuilding after a setback, stepping into a new season, or trying to show up more boldly in your life or business, it all starts with the habits you practice.

Perfection won't build you but discipline will. Confidence grows every time you honor your commitment, even when it's uncomfortable because that's where the transformation happens. Confidence isn't loud. It doesn't scream. But it *shows up*—daily.

The Confidence Myth: You're Not Born With It, You Build It

Let's dismantle this myth right now: a lot of people think confidence is a trait—you either have it or you don't. That's false. Confidence isn't a personality trait. It's a *behavior*. It's built through action, repetition, and intentional choice. It's not about faking it till you make it. It's about proving to yourself that you *can*, one step at a time.

When you show up for yourself over and over again, even in the smallest ways, your inner belief system starts to shift. You begin to trust yourself. You start thinking, *"If I could do that yesterday, I can do it again today."* That's what makes your confidence unshakeable. Not the external applause, but the internal consistency.

Why Habits Matter More Than Hype

Motivation might get you started, but it won't carry you through the days when life feels heavy. Hype fades. But habits? Habits anchor you.

Think of habits as confidence deposits. Every time you do something that aligns with your purpose—whether it's journaling, stretching, meal prepping, praying, or simply drinking your water—you're depositing into your *confidence account*. Over time, your account grows, and you stop operating from insecurity and start leading from identity.

Let me be real with you—I didn't rebuild my life or confidence overnight. After experiencing loss of my significant other, work burnout, and walking away from a career that no longer served me, I had to rediscover my *own worth*. And it wasn't a big moment that changed me—it was the small ones. It was the habits I committed to in the *dark*, when no one else was watching.

My Personal Morning Routine: The Confidence Kickoff

I don't believe in chasing perfection—but I do believe in setting the tone. My morning routine isn't about checking off a list. It's about alignment. It's about starting the day with intention so that I can lead myself before I lead anyone else. What I do in that first hour grounds me, centers me, and reminds me of the woman I've committed to becoming.

Let me walk you through my morning routine—not because it's perfect, but because it's purposeful. These habits help me start the day with clarity, energy, and confidence. They aren't about hype—they're about alignment.

- **Gratitude First** - Before I even touch my phone, I take a moment to speak out loud what I'm grateful for. Not just in my mind—I *speak* it. There's something powerful about hearing your own voice declare what's working in your life. Gratitude shifts the focus from what's missing to what's already meaningful. It softens anxiety and opens your heart.

  Then I reach for what I call my *mindset fuel*—I first pray, then either read a passage of scripture, meditate on something uplifting, or listen to a podcast or music that speaks to my soul. This is intentional. I don't scroll. I don't start my day with the noise of the world. I get to decide what pours into me first. I protect my peace before I give my energy to anyone else.

- **Speak Life** – I say my affirmations out loud. Not silently. I need to hear my own voice remind me who I am and what I'm capable of. This part of my routine is speaking life over myself. Out loud. Not in a whisper. I need to hear the sound of my own authority. These are more than just phrases. They're declarations. They remind me of my identity, my vision, and my truth—even when my circumstances don't match up yet.

  Here are six affirmations I say daily:

1. **"I am destined for greatness."**
2. **"I am naturally dynamic and confident."**
3. **"I've got what it takes to win in every area of my life."**
4. **"I am beautiful."**

5. **"I am healthy and healed."**

6. **"I am a visionary."**

And when I'm really in alignment and feeling bold, I add the big one # 7:

"I am a MULTI-MILLIONAIRE. Time just hasn't caught up with me yet."

Yes, I speak it. Because I believe in vision. I believe in bold declarations. I believe in calling it before I see it. My dreams for the *Convicted to Grow* brand are massive and impactful—and that starts with me affirming what I already know to be true in my spirit.

- **Move My Body** – Movement is non-negotiable. It doesn't have to be a full workout. Sometimes it's a walk. Sometimes it's stretching, dancing in the mirror, or a few minutes of intentional movement to get my blood flowing.

  But what matters is that I *move*. Because when I move my body, I move my energy. I shift my mindset. I signal to myself that I'm alive, in charge, and capable. It also helps me release whatever tension I might be carrying from the day before. Movement reminds me that I'm not stagnant—and neither is my growth.

  This isn't about losing weight or chasing some physical ideal. For me, especially during my personal health journey, movement became sacred. When I made the decision to take my health seriously—fueling my body differently, starting intermittent fasting, getting intentional about what I consumed physically and mentally—it wasn't about appearance. It was about reclaiming my energy, my glow, and my confidence. Every drop of sweat became a statement: *I choose me.*

- **Quick Wins and Reflections** – I knock out one small task to build momentum. Even if it's Before the world demands my attention, I knock out one small task that gives me momentum. Maybe I will meal prep.. Maybe I respond to one email I've been avoiding. Maybe I will review my planner and check something off. It doesn't have to be a big win—it just needs to remind me that I'm capable and in motion. That small action sets the tone for everything else.

When I have more time, I journal. This isn't a strict routine, but when I feel something stirring in my spirit—whether it's a fear, a vision, or a word of encouragement—I get it out on paper. Journaling has helped me process deep emotions during my grief, articulate goals during my rebuilding season, and celebrate the moments I might've otherwise overlooked.

There's power in pausing to reflect, especially when you're on a journey of healing and elevation. Your journal becomes proof of progress—written evidence that you're not where you used to be.

This morning routine isn't about being perfect. It's about showing up for the version of me I'm committed to becoming. It creates a rhythm of ownership and alignment that helps me start my day from a place of peace—not pressure.

It also reminds me of my *why*. Why I speak. Why I coach. Why I write. Why I move forward—even when it's hard. When you create a morning routine rooted in gratitude, movement, mindset, and vision, you stop waking up to survive—and start waking up to *lead*.

You don't need my exact routine. But you do need *yours*. Something that's rooted in who you are and who you're becoming. Your routine doesn't need to be long. It just needs to be *intentional*.

The Power of Micro-Habits

You don't need an entire lifestyle overhaul to build confidence. You just need *micro-habits* that compound over time. Think of micro-habits as small, non-negotiable actions that you commit to daily—like brushing your teeth but for your mindset.

Here are a few that can change everything:

- **Make your bed** – It sets the tone for order.
- **Speak one affirmation aloud** – Just one.
- **Look yourself in the mirror and smile** – It sounds cheesy, but it works.
- **Complete one task you've been avoiding** – Action kills anxiety.
- **Celebrate small wins** – Don't wait for big milestones.

These aren't life-changing in isolation, but done daily? They become evidence. Evidence that you're reliable. Evidence that you're growing. Evidence that you're not who you used to be.

Discipline Over Drama

Let's keep it real—there will be days when you just don't feel like it. Days when the alarm goes off and you want to hit snooze on your purpose. Days when scrolling through your phone seems easier than scrolling through your vision board. Days when you question everything you're building. And that's exactly when the real decision shows up: **Do I want results, or do I want routines?**

Confidence isn't a one-time pep talk—it's a practice. And practice isn't always pretty. It means showing up when you're tired. Choosing progress over perfection. Repeating what works until it becomes who you are.

This is where discipline steps in—not because it's glamorous, but because it builds grit. Grit is what gets you through the quiet seasons, the slow days, and the moments when no one claps. It's what strengthens your voice when self-doubt tries to steal it.

I've had mornings where tears hit the journal before ink did. I've coached clients while holding back my own pain. There have been days when my confidence felt silent—but my habits still spoke. The moment I returned to my rhythm—my morning routine, my affirmations, my prayer, my movement—I remembered who I was. And sometimes, remembering is more powerful than motivation.

Build It Before You Need It

Confidence isn't something you scramble to find when life gets hard—it's something you build in advance. Just like a house needs a solid foundation before the storm hits, your habits are the concrete beneath your confidence. You don't wait for the rain to start laying bricks.

If you only feel confident when everything's going right, that's not confidence—that's comfort. True confidence shows up when things get messy. It's the kind that stands tall in uncertainty because it's been trained in stillness.

When you develop daily disciplines that stretch your mindset, strengthen your focus, and align your actions, you're building muscle—emotional, mental, spiritual. And that kind of strength? It's unshakable. Not because life is easy, but because you've done the work to be ready.

Final Thoughts

Confidence isn't built under the spotlight—it's built behind the scenes.

It's formed in the quiet moments when you choose growth over comfort. It's shaped in the small decisions no one applauds. It's anchored in the habits that remind you of who you are—even when life tries to make you forget.

So the next time you ask, *"How do I become more confident?"*

Check your habits.

Audit your daily choices.

Look closely at how you show up for *you*.

Because the most confident version of you? They already exist within. You don't need to chase them—you need to *uncover* them. And that begins by building a lifestyle that supports their rise—one morning, one habit, one aligned decision at a time.

Start today.

Stay consistent.

And watch who you become.

Action Steps

Let's move from inspiration to implementation. You don't need a to-do list—you need *alignment*.

Here's your confidence-building assignment:

1. **Choose 3 Confidence-Building Habits You Can Start Tomorrow**
   Pick small, clear, and sustainable actions that align with who you're becoming. These habits should support the version of you you're working toward—not the one you're trying to grow out of.
   Examples: Say one affirmation aloud and repeat daily, move your body for 15-20 minutes, review your goals each morning, and focus on one action that moves you closer to those goals.

2. **Commit for 7 Days—No Breaks, No Excuses**
   This isn't a sprint—it's a cycle. If 21 or 30 days feels overwhelming, start with 7. Then repeat it. Build momentum in manageable chunks. A 7-day commitment on *repeat* becomes a habit before you know it.

3. **Track Your Energy and Mindset**
   Each night, reflect with a quick journal prompt: How did I show up for myself today? What shifted in my energy or mindset?

4. Celebrate the Small Wins

Confidence is built in tiny victories. Don't wait for a milestone—acknowledge the progress you're making right now.

Examples of small wins:

- You got out of bed when you didn't feel like it.
- You drank your water and nourished your body.
- You said your affirmation even when self-doubt whispered louder.
- You showed up to the meeting, the workout, or the call—on time and fully present.
- You chose faith over fear, even for a moment.
- You hit "post" and shared your content online.
- You set a boundary. You said no. You protected your peace.

Small doesn't mean insignificant. Every time you honor your growth, you reinforce your confidence.

5. If You Miss a Day, Don't Start Over—Pick Up Where You Left Off

Growth isn't about streaks—it's about *returning*. It's easy to fall into the trap of "I missed a day, so I have to start all over." But confidence isn't built through punishment. It's built through *permission*—the permission to get back up without guilt.

Resilience is created in the comeback, not in never missing a step. One missed day doesn't erase your progress. It's not about being perfect—it's about being *present* and *persistent*.

When life gets messy or momentum slows down:

Take a breath and pause for the cause.

Give yourself permission to pause without guilt. Sometimes, a moment of stillness is more productive than pushing through on empty. Your pause is not a setback—it's a sacred space to breathe, reset, and realign.

Re-center yourself.

Ask yourself: : *What do I need at this moment?* Return to your why. Reflect on the version of you you're becoming. Sometimes, clarity comes not from doing more, but from getting still and remembering your purpose.

Return to your habit with grace.

There's no need to punish yourself for missing a day. Shame stalls growth—grace restores it. Pick back up where you left off, not from a place of pressure, but from a place of *power*. Your ability to realign is proof of your resilience.

Keep going—your progress still counts. Every step forward matters. Stay rooted in your habits, respect the process, and believe this truth: you're not just growing—you're becoming the version of yourself you were always meant to be.

Part IV:
The Commitment

Chapter 10:
Progress Doesn't Require Perfection

By now, you've acknowledged your setbacks, confronted your fears, and started the hard work of rebuilding your confidence and stepping into boldness. You've pulled back the layers, started back reconnecting to your why, and begun rising into the version of yourself you were always meant to be.

But here's the truth: once you've been **convicted to grow**, you must make the decision to be **committed to growing**—every single day. Growth is a daily thing.

The work doesn't stop at awareness. Confidence isn't sustained through inspiration alone. Now, it's about intention. Daily alignment. Ownership. It's about committing to the habits, mindset, and choices that protect your progress and push you toward your purpose. This part of the journey isn't about hype—it's about discipline. It's about doing the work, even when no one is clapping, and especially when self doubt creeps back in.

Let's go ahead and release the pressure right now: you do not need to be perfect to grow. You don't need to have it all figured out, all mapped out, or all cleaned up to move forward. If you've been delaying your next step because you think you're not polished enough, ready enough, or worthy enough, let this chapter be your permission to move anyway.

Progress has nothing to do with perfection. In fact, perfection is often the enemy of progress. It keeps you frozen in place, always preparing, always overthinking, always trying to make the next move "just right."

But let me tell you something real: bold, lasting growth is built in the mess. It's forged in the unfiltered moments, the small daily choices, and the quiet victories that nobody else sees. It doesn't look perfect. It looks *real*.

The Perfection Trap

We live in a world that rewards appearance. It celebrates the highlight reel, the polished brand, the flawless finish. And because of that, so many people fall into the trap of waiting to be perfect before they act. Before they launch. Before they speak. Before they lead.

Here's the truth: if you're always waiting to be perfect, you'll always be waiting.

Perfectionism is fear dressed up as ambition. It's the fear of being judged. The fear of not being good enough. The fear of failing in front of others. But here's what I want you to remember—real growth doesn't happen in the planning room. It happens in the field. In the action. In the doing.

You do not need to be the best to begin. You just need to *begin*.

Give Yourself Permission to Be In Progress

Let this be your gentle but firm reminder: You are allowed to be a work in progress and still make an impact. You can be healing and still helping. You can be learning and still leading. You can be growing and still showing up.

There is so much power in showing up as you are, not as you think you have to be.

One of the most confident things you can do is to keep moving while you're evolving. Why? Because perfection is a moving target. Every time you think you've arrived, the standard shifts. But progress?

Progress says, "Look at how far you've come." Progress builds momentum. Progress reminds you that you're becoming.

I remember when I first set out to launch my podcast. It was a vision that came to me back in 2022, right before my significant other passed away. He encouraged me, saying, "You have everything you need, just do it." But I kept feeling unready, and after his passing, grief became my new reason to delay. Even as I healed and prayed for direction in 2023, I realized the only thing holding me back was me.

I invested in all the equipment—microphones, lights, you name it—thinking that preparation would replace action. But in reality, I was using perfectionism as a shield from starting. When I finally set a public launch date—February 24, 2024—I knew I had to commit. Even then, I kept telling my audience, "Hey everyone, I'm learning as I go, so bear with me." That journey taught me that growth happens through execution, not perfect preparation. And each episode became a testament to stepping out of my own way, embracing the process, and realizing that I had it in me all along.

And now, here we are, nearly 18 months into the Convicted to Grow Podcast, and the growth is astounding. When I compare my first episode to episode 60, the transformation is undeniable—not just in how I speak or interview, but in how I carry myself on camera. Looking back, those first ten episodes were filled with nerves and filler words. Now, each recording starts with confidence; I look through the lens and connect with my audience, knowing that each rep has built this presence.

To anyone looking to launch a YouTube channel, a podcast, or a business: I'm living proof that showing up consistently matters. Even when I had only two views, no likes, and no shares, I kept going. Don't let validation from others define your journey. If you believe in yourself and your brand, and you know you have something magical to share with the world, keep pushing. The best is yet to come—so don't cheat your gift. Keep striving, and watch how things start manifesting in your favor

Start Messy. Start Anyway.

Too many dreams are stuck in notebooks. Too many ideas are trapped in the minds of brilliant people who are afraid to start messy. But here's what you need to know: your imperfect action will teach you more than perfect planning ever will.

Confidence grows through doing. Through feedback. Through falling forward. Every mistake becomes a lesson. Every setback becomes a setup for resilience. Every awkward attempt is a seed planted in your future success.

You don't learn confidence by waiting for the perfect conditions. You learn it by trusting yourself enough to take the next step, even when it's uncomfortable. Especially when it's uncomfortable.

As a confidence coach, I've guided countless clients through their journeys of rebuilding their lives, careers, and businesses—much like my own ongoing journey. One common thread I see, especially among my female clients, is the pursuit of perfection. Often, this perfectionism stems from a desire for external validation—trying to meet the expectations of those around them, or fearing judgment from their inner circles. But striving for perfection can stifle growth. I often tell my clients that if they can't be authentic, especially on social media, it might be time to start fresh and attract a new, organic audience who resonates with their true message. Your vision and purpose are bigger than any local validation. If you keep confining yourself to the expectations of those who already know you, you'll never step into your full potential and shine like the diamond you are.

Replace Pressure with Grace

Let's talk about replacing pressure with grace. Many of us carry the weight of unrealistic expectations, beating ourselves up for not being further along and comparing our timelines to others. But the truth is, you are right on time. I call it divine alignment and divine assignment—timing is everything.

One of the biggest challenges I see, especially with my clients, is the trap of comparison. You're measuring your progress against someone else's chapter without knowing the full story—the sacrifices, the struggles, the journey. Maybe you share the same age, interests, or industry, and you wonder why they're ahead. But it's not about who's ahead; it's about your unique timing and path.

Procrastination, hesitation, self-doubt—these can all delay our journey, and that's okay. Grace isn't about lowering your standards; it's about honoring your humanity. Progress isn't linear—some days you'll leap forward, some days you'll take small steps, and some days you'll stand still.

Whether you're leaping, stepping, or pausing, you're still on the path of growth. Give yourself the grace to breathe, pivot, and try again without shame or guilt. The grace you give yourself will be the key to staying in the race, rebuilding, and rising stronger than ever before.

The Power of Micro-Momentum

Progress isn't about waiting until everything is polished, perfect, or publicly applauded. It's built in the quiet, consistent decisions no one sees. The moments when you wake up and choose not to give up. When you make your bed to regain a sense of control. When you hit "publish" on that post—even though you questioned if anyone would care. When you say "yes" to the opportunity, even as fear tries to convince you to shrink. These aren't just small tasks—they're powerful declarations that you're committed to the version of yourself that's growing, not the one stuck in fear or procrastination

That's the power of micro-momentum. It's not loud. It's not flashy. But it's faithful. And faithful movement—no matter how small—is what separates dreamers from doers. When you stop waiting for the breakthrough moment and start honoring the small ones, something shifts. You begin to grow with grace. You recognize that progress is happening—not because it's perfect, but because it's in motion. You don't need to have it all figured out to move forward. You just need to move—and trust that your commitment will make you stronger.

I've lived this. When I finally launched the *Convicted to Grow* Podcast, I had everything I needed—except the belief that I was ready. The mic, the setup, the content were all there. But fear had me frozen. I recorded the first episode five times. My voice trembled. I was grieving, still healing, and second-guessing myself every step of the way. But I pressed "publish" anyway. That moment didn't come with a round of applause—but it came with peace. It was me choosing to grow in real time. Choosing to show up, imperfect but committed.

Be Proud of Where You Are

Pause and take a look at where you are right now. Think about the version of you who once dreamed of being exactly here. You may not be where you want to be just yet, but you are certainly not where you started and that's something to be proud of. The version of you from a year ago, five years ago, or even six months ago would be in awe of what you've pushed through. We don't often give ourselves enough credit for the quiet strength it takes to keep moving forward, especially when the progress doesn't come with praise or recognition.

I've been there. After losing my partner, I found myself in a space where I had to decide whether I was going to stay stuck in my grief or grow through it. I had the tools, the setup, the support—but internally, I felt empty. Starting over didn't feel empowering at first. It felt like walking through fog, trying to find clarity while carrying pain. I kept thinking I had to be fully healed or completely ready before taking the next step. But I realized that healing and progress happen at the same time. You don't need to wait for perfection to move—you just need the courage to begin.

And that's what you've done. That's what makes your journey so powerful.

So many people never give themselves that chance. They talk themselves out of purpose because they can't guarantee perfection. But not you. You said yes—even when everything in you wanted to wait. You decided to rebuild, to try again, to lean into your calling even if it didn't feel easy. And that decision? That's proof of growth.

Don't overlook this season. Don't minimize the work you've done just because the results haven't gone viral. Your consistency is building something. Your resilience is inspiring someone. Your decision to keep going day by day is the evidence that progress is possible for anyone willing to do the work.

This version of you isn't the final one—but they are becoming something remarkable and that is worth being proud of.

Final Thoughts

Visualize the version of you who's already walking in the success you're working toward. Not just the milestones, but the mindset. The clarity. The calm. The confidence. Picture how you speak, how you lead, how you move with intention and conviction. That version of you isn't far off—it's already within you, waiting to be embodied. That vision isn't a fantasy—it's a blueprint. A reminder that everything you're doing right now—every habit, every decision, every moment of courage—is building the reality you once dreamed of. So stop shrinking your vision to match your current season. Start stretching your mindset to match the future that's calling you.

The commitment to grow isn't about flawless execution—it's about *faithful movement.* It's the decision to show up as you are, not as who you think the world expects you to be. It's giving yourself the freedom to be both in progress and impactful. You don't need to have it all figured out to start making a difference.

You don't need to prove anything to anyone. This journey isn't about performing—it's about being present. Present with your purpose. Present with your process. Present with your power.

So take the step. Stumble if you have to. Shift directions if needed. But don't sit on your assignment just because it doesn't look perfect yet. You are not behind. You are not broken. You are not disqualified. You are evolving. You are becoming. You are being refined—not erased.

Let that truth settle in your spirit today—and carry it with you every day forward.

Action Steps

You don't need to have it all figured out—just take the next aligned step. Here are four simple ways to put Chapter 10 into motion:

1. Visualize Your Future Self

Take 5 quiet minutes today to picture the version of you who's fully walking in confidence and clarity.
Ask: *What decisions does that version of me make? What energy do they carry?*

2. Identify One Area Where You're Over-Perfecting

Where are you holding back because you're waiting to "get it right"? Choose one thing you've been overthinking and do it. Post the content. Start the conversation. Press "publish." Progress doesn't wait for perfection..

3. Celebrate One Small Win

Write down one thing you've done recently—even something small—that reflects progress.
Say to yourself: *"That counted. That was progress."*

4. Speak This Truth Over Yourself

"I am in progress, not behind. I am becoming, not broken. I am free to grow, not obligated to prove."
Repeat it when doubt creeps in.

Chapter 11:
Aligning Your Life with Meaningful Impact

There comes a moment in your growth journey when the internal work must begin to reflect externally. You've been healing, rebuilding, reclaiming your voice, and reconnecting with your boldness. Now, it's time to align your life with the impact you were born to make. Because impact isn't something that just happens—it's something you build, intentionally, and it starts with living in alignment.

Alignment means living a life where your values, voice, vision, and actions are all moving in the same direction. It's the decision to no longer chase success that doesn't satisfy, and instead, create a life of purpose-driven impact that fulfills you from the inside out.

I spent years checking all the boxes—climbing corporate ladders, exceeding metrics, collecting titles, and performing at a high level. On the outside, it looked like I was winning. I had the job, the benefits, the respect. But inside? I was slowly disappearing. I was exhausted from performing for everyone else's version of success while silencing the voice inside me that kept asking, *"Is this it?"*

For me, alignment didn't begin until I stopped performing and started being.

I'll never forget the day it hit me. I had just logged off a high-level Zoom call with other executive leaders—camera off, mic muted, still holding the title of President of Talent Acquisition. From the outside, I was at the top of my game. I was leading with excellence, managing high-stakes recruitment, building business development pipelines, training teams, and carrying the weight of deliverables that never seemed to slow down. I had what many would call a "dream role"—but I was silently drowning.

I sat in silence after that meeting and whispered to myself, *"I don't even enjoy what I do anymore."*

And just like that... I knew. That whisper was the beginning of my realignment.

I had been working 16-hour days, trying to meet impossible expectations—most of which I placed on myself. I never asked for help. I didn't feel like I could. The imposter syndrome had convinced me that perfection was the price I had to pay to keep my seat at the table. And let's be honest—when you're a woman in leadership, the pressure to overperform while appearing unshaken is real. We suffer in silence because we fear that asking for help will make us look weak, unqualified, or incapable.

But the truth is, I was exhausted. I wasn't just tired from the work—I was tired from pretending that I was ok. Tired of showing up polished and high-performing, while my peace and purpose were quietly slipping through the cracks. I was shrinking behind the scenes just to maintain the image of having it all together.

That moment—sitting there after that Zoom call—wasn't the end. It was my wake-up call. My permission to stop chasing a version of success that no longer aligned with who I was becoming. That's when I realized: if the cost of success is losing yourself, it's too expensive.

So I made the decision to shift. Not all at once, but intentionally. I began to redefine what success looked like for me. I started listening to the voice I had silenced for too long. I got honest about what I needed—and what I was no longer willing to carry alone. It's not about walking away from leadership—it's about leading yourself first. It's not about proving you can do it all—it's about honoring what's sustainable, purposeful, and aligned.

If you're reading this and you've had your own *"I don't even enjoy this anymore"* moment—don't ignore it. That's not a failure. That's your inner truth trying to pull you into something greater. You don't have to break to begin again. You just have to be willing to stop suffering in silence and start leading from a place of wholeness. That's your invitation to realign, to redefine, and to rise stronger.

Because you deserve a version of success that doesn't require you to lose yourself to achieve it. It was the first time I gave myself permission to tell the truth: I had outgrown who I was pretending to be. My calling was no longer in the comfort of what I knew. And as scary as that realization was, it was also freeing. I wasn't lost—I was being led into something new. Purpose was calling me to stop performing and start showing up fully as myself. I stopped chasing validation and started listening to my own voice. I stopped managing burnout and started creating boundaries. I let go of the version of success that looked good but felt empty—and began rebuilding a life and business that felt aligned with who I really am.

What Alignment Really Looks Like

What does alignment really look like? It's not about having a perfect plan; it's about having an honest one. It's about doing the deep internal work to understand what truly matters to you, what drains you, and what energizes you. It's about recognizing whether you're showing up out of obligation or calling.

I remember when I was at the peak of my burnout phase. It took a toll on me—mentally, emotionally, physically, and spiritually. I didn't have time to pray, exercise, or even practice basic self-care. I was chasing success but losing myself in the process.

One day, it all came to a head. I found myself in urgent care, convinced something was wrong with me. The pressure on my chest felt like a ton of bricks. Even as I lay there, hooked up to machines, I was still checking emails, scheduling interviews, and talking to candidates. I was so caught up in the grind that I couldn't even recognize the red flags my own body was waving.

After a few hours, the doctor came in with the diagnosis: stress. My heart and chest was fine, but everything else wasn't. I was told to take it easy, get proper sleep, eat better, and exercise. But even then, I rationalized that a few days off would fix everything. It didn't.

That moment was my wake-up call. I realized I was sacrificing my health, my peace, and my purpose for a salary. The truth is, even with a great paycheck, if you're not in alignment, you're just existing—not living. And when I finally took that leap, stepped away, and started focusing on what truly aligned with my purpose, everything changed. That's when I realized my voice, my gift to inspire and uplift others to grow and elevate, was my true calling.

When you're in alignment, your decisions feel lighter, your confidence rises, and you stop chasing validation. You start attracting opportunities that align with who you truly are. And even when life threw another curveball—like losing my significant other to a heart attack shortly after me walking away from my job—I was still on the path of alignment but it was more personal as I started looking at life differently. Tomorrow is not promised so focus on today. Too many people leave this world every second unexpectedly. We don't know our expiration date but while we here recognize your potential and purpose because you matter. My journey now serves as a testament that even after setbacks, you can rise stronger and more purposeful than ever.

So, take that time for a clarity check. Ask yourself: Are you genuinely happy? Are you living in alignment with your purpose? Life is too short to live any other way. When you stop chasing validation and start embracing alignment, you open yourself up to a life where your yes comes with peace and your no is a complete sentence, free from guilt.

Tools to Build Alignment

Alignment doesn't just happen—it's built with intention. It's the result of clarity, consistency, and courageous choices. If you want to live and lead with authenticity and confidence, there are three essential tools that will keep you grounded: **your values, self-reflection,** and **boundaries.**

Tool 1: Clarify Your Core Values

Your values are your personal GPS. They tell you what to protect, what to pursue, and what no longer fits. When you know what you value, decisions become clearer, your "yes" gets stronger, and your "no" becomes more confident. But when your actions don't match your values, you start to feel misaligned—stretched thin, restless, or even resentful.

Ask yourself:

- What do I value more than anything?
- Do my choices reflect those values?
- Are my work, relationships, and daily habits aligned with what I say matters?

When I realigned my life with my values—**confidence**, **impact, gratitude, leadership, community** and **growth**—everything shifted. I stopped accepting opportunities that silenced my voice or didn't know my worth. I walked away from rooms that only tolerated me. I started building programs and community from a place of passion, not pressure.

Living in alignment with your values gives your life direction and depth.

Tool 2: Practice Consistent Self-Reflection

Self-reflection is how you stay honest with yourself. It's the space where you check in with what feels good, what feels off, and what needs to shift. Whether it's journaling, prayer, meditation, or quiet walks—reflection keeps you connected to your purpose.

Ask yourself regularly:

- What's energizing me right now?
- What's draining me?
- What am I avoiding that needs my attention?

You don't have to wait until you're burned out to realign. Reflection gives you the clarity to course-correct before things fall apart. It helps you move with intention instead of reacting out of obligation.

Tool 3: Set Boundaries That Protect Your Alignment

Values show you what matters. Reflection reveals your truth. But boundaries are what protect it.

Without boundaries, even the most purpose-driven person can end up overextended, overwhelmed, and out of alignment. Boundaries are not selfish—they're strategic. They guard your time, energy, focus, and peace.

Ask yourself:

- Where am I constantly feeling stretched or resentful?
- What am I saying "yes" to that I need to release?
- What boundaries need to be set or reinforced?

For me, that meant learning to say no without overexplaining, carving out space for rest without guilt, and no longer allowing urgency to dictate my priorities.The more I honored my boundaries, the more aligned and confident I became.

Boundaries aren't about keeping people out—they're about keeping your purpose and energy protected.

You can't live with meaningful impact if you're constantly betraying your values, ignoring your inner voice, or abandoning yourself to be liked. Alignment isn't perfection—it's permission to live in truth.

Let your **values** lead, let **reflection** guide, and let **boundaries** protect the life you're building.

Saying No to What No Longer Serves You

There was a moment when I could've chosen comfort—the title, the salary, the benefits, and the familiar rhythm of what I knew best. On the outside, it looked like success. But inside, my purpose was being suffocated, my voice was being muted, and my gifts were cramped into a space too small for who I was becoming.

I wrestled with the decision for weeks. Fear whispered, *"What if you leave and fail? What if you lose everything?"* But faith spoke louder: *"What if you leave and rise?"*

When I turned in my resignation, I didn't have a backup plan. I consulted with my significant other, who supported me 100%, and I took that leap of faith. I didn't have a roadmap, but I had vision. My vision was bigger than my reality, and my purpose was greater than my zip code. The peace I felt was everything.

That decision wasn't just about leaving a job; it was about refusing to stay in spaces where my purpose couldn't breathe, grow, or lead. While entrepreneurship came with its own set of challenges—grit, growth, and a disciplined mindset—every step made sense. That "no" created space for the most aligned "yes" of my life.

Since then, I've had over 20 paid speaking engagements, worked with numerous one-on-one clients on confidence building and business strategy, and built the Convicted to Grow community. I've stepped into rooms I once thought were beyond my reach and stood out as a beacon of resilience and growth.

Without that courageous "no," there wouldn't be a Convicted to Grow. That choice has led me to a life of impact, vision, and alignment that my old title could never contain. It's been a journey of meeting the best version of myself and living out the conviction to grow every single day.

Ask yourself: What am I holding onto that no longer serves my growth? What would happen if I said no to the things that confine me and yes to the opportunities that could elevate me?

Your next breakthrough might just be on the other side of a courageous "no."

Leading a Life That Leaves a Legacy

When your life is aligned, your impact multiplies. You're no longer just busy—you're effective. You're not simply working—you're building something that lasts. And that legacy isn't measured by titles or timelines, but by the lives you touch and the purpose you fulfill along the way.

Alignment transforms the everyday grind into a purposeful journey. When you begin saying no to what no longer serves you, you create space for what truly matters. You're not just chasing goals—you're laying a foundation. You're building something that others will benefit from long after your task is done. That's the power of a legacy. It's not always loud, but it always leaves a mark.

Legacy isn't about grand gestures or monumental achievements. It's about the consistent, intentional actions—done in alignment—that create ripples of change. It's about showing up authentically, living in purpose, and giving others permission to do the same just by watching how you lead your life.

As you continue aligning your life for meaningful impact, keep this in mind: Your legacy is built in the moments you choose alignment over convenience, purpose over popularity, and impact over impression.

So pause and reflect:

- What legacy are you building with the choices you make today?
- How are your daily actions shaping the impact you want to leave behind?
- Are you mentoring others through how you show up—without even saying a word?
- Are you showing your children, your clients, your team what it means to live boldly—not perfectly?

Alignment isn't about impressing people. It's about inspiring them—through your presence, your purpose, and your bold authenticity.

When I think about the people who impacted me most—mentors, leaders, teachers—it wasn't their resumes that moved me. It was their conviction. It was the way they showed up, aligned with their truth, connected to purpose, and in tune with the season I was in. That's what stuck. That's what shaped me.

And that's what legacy is all about.

Conducting Your Alignment Audit

Let's get practical. Alignment starts with *awareness*—not just of where you want to go, but of where you currently stand. This audit is a moment of truth, not judgment. It's about getting clear on what's working, what's weighing you down, and what needs to shift so your life reflects your purpose and peace.

Clarify Your Core Values

If everything else was stripped away—titles, tasks, expectations—what values would you refuse to compromise? Write down your top five. These values should guide how you show up, what you prioritize, and what you release.

Assess Your Time

Look at how you're spending your time—not just in theory, but in reality. Does your calendar reflect what you say matters most? Are your daily rhythms supporting your growth or draining your energy?

Evaluate Your Circle

Take inventory of your environment. Are the people around you aligned with your growth—or pulling you off course? Are you surrounded by encouragement and accountability or expectations and comparison?

Reflect on Your Work

Does the work you're doing honor your gifts, your passion, and your calling? You don't have to overhaul everything overnight—but ask yourself: *What small adjustments could bring me closer to alignment in how I work and serve?*

Listen to Your Body

Your body carries wisdom. Pay attention to the signals—tight shoulders, racing thoughts, drained energy. Where in your life are you experiencing tension? And what choices tend to restore your peace?

Alignment isn't a one-time decision—it's a lifestyle and it starts with honesty. The more you reflect, the more clarity you gain. And the more courageously you act on that clarity, the more your life begins to feel like *you*—on purpose, in flow, and in integrity.

The Power of Aligned Shifts

There comes a moment when growth demands more than just motivation—it demands a shift. Not just any shift, but an *aligned* one. The kind that calls you to pivot, to realign, and to move in the direction of purpose—even when it's uncomfortable. Aligned shifts don't always come with clarity at first. Sometimes, they begin with a whisper. A restlessness. A tug on your spirit that says, *"This isn't it anymore."*

Aligned shifts are not about drastic moves—they're about intentional pivots that bring you closer to the life you're called to live. They may feel risky. They may disrupt your comfort. But they will always lead you toward your truth.

So ask yourself:

- Where am I being nudged to shift?
- What am I clinging to that no longer fits who I'm becoming?
- What might open up if I gave myself permission to pivot, even without all the answers?

Aligned shifts are how you rebuild.

Aligned shifts are how you rise.

And aligned shifts are how you reclaim the life, leadership, and legacy you were always meant for.

Final Thoughts

You weren't created to hustle your way into purpose. You were designed to live and lead from alignment. When your life reflects your values, your vision, and your voice—you become unstoppable.

What the world needs most isn't a flawless version of you—it needs the real you. Present. Aligned. Unapologetically bold.

So if something in your life feels off—don't ignore it. *Explore it. Question it. Adjust it.* Give yourself permission to choose differently. To make decisions that reflect not just who you've been—but who you're becoming.

You can't fake alignment. But when you find it, you'll feel it—deep in your body, in your relationships, in your business, and in your confidence. Things start to click. Peace replaces pressure. Purpose replaces performance and clarity becomes your new standard.

Action Steps

Alignment is not a one-time decision—it's a daily practice. Here are five focused steps to help you live and lead in alignment with your purpose:

1. Audit Your Alignment
Identify one area of your life—work, relationships, habits, or mindset—that feels out of sync.
  Ask: *What feels heavy or forced? What feels true and life-giving?*

2. Revisit Your Core Values
Write down your top 3–5 non-negotiable values.
  Then ask: *Does how I live, work, and lead reflect what I say matters most?*

3. Make One Aligned Shift
Choose one meaningful change you can make this week—no matter how small.
  Example: Say no to something draining, change a routine, or speak up where you've been quiet.

4. Set a Boundary That Honors Your Peace
Where do you need to pause, pull back, or stop overcommitting?
  Protect your energy so your purpose can flourish.

5. Say It Out Loud
Affirm your alignment daily:
  "I align my life with purpose, peace, and power. I release what no longer serves me and boldly step into what does."

You owe it to yourself to align with the version of you that's been waiting to be fully seen, fully heard, and fully expressed. Your next level isn't waiting on perfection. It's waiting on permission. You don't have to get it all right. You just have to get honest, take action, and stay committed to becoming the most aligned version of you.

Chapter 12:
Leading with Conviction

There comes a moment in every person's life when they must decide: Will I live on autopilot, or will I lead—with conviction?

Leadership isn't about having a title, a corner office, or a big platform. Leadership is influence. And the first place you're called to lead is your own life. You are the leader of your mindset, the steward of your habits and the driver of your direction. The way you choose to grow mentally, emotionally, spiritually, and professionally is leadership.

This movement, *Convicted to Grow*, isn't just a brand or catchy name. It's a call to live and lead from a deeper place. A place of clarity, of courage, of being fully anchored in who you are and where you're going. Conviction isn't about being right or rigid. It's about being rooted. It's a call to lead and live from a place of alignment and accountability—to be convicted in the way you show up, grow, and elevate in every area of your life, career, and business.

From Compliance to Conviction: My Story

For years, I led from a place of performance. In corporate leadership, I held high-level titles and managed major teams. I hit the goals, led the meetings, trained the teams. From the outside, I was winning. But inside? I was conforming. Leading by policy. Executing expectations. I was checking boxes—but losing myself. I wasn't taking care of myself like the leader I was.

My wake-up call didn't come with fanfare. It came in layers: through entrepreneurship, through navigating grief after losing my significant other, through the weight loss journey that forced me to face my discipline—or lack of it. It came in the silence after the Zoom calls, the heaviness after 16-hour workdays, the realization that I was performing instead of being.

My conviction began with one honest moment: *I have to do better.* And if I know better, I'm now responsible to lead better. I made a decision to lead myself first—in health, in healing, in my business, and in my purpose. That choice changed everything.

What Does It Mean to Lead with Conviction?

To lead with conviction means you stop waiting to feel ready—and start showing up from a place of truth. You speak when it's easier to stay silent. You make purpose-driven decisions, not popularity-based ones. You don't shrink to fit in or shift just to be liked.

You lead from a steady internal compass, not external applause. And you don't lead because you have all the answers—you lead because you've decided to stay committed.

The Marks of a Conviction-Driven Leader

- **Clarity of Purpose** – You know what you stand for. You lead from mission, not mood.

- **Courage to Be Unpopular** – You're willing to stand alone to stay aligned.

- **Consistency in Action** – Your walk matches your talk.

- **Compassion and Accountability** – You lead with empathy, but you don't lower the bar.

- **Confidence in Your Voice** – You don't have to dominate the room. Your words carry weight because they're backed by truth.

A Client Transformation: Finding Her Voice

One of my clients came to me feeling lost in her leadership role. On paper, she had everything—an impressive title, a solid team, and years of experience. But beneath the surface, she was struggling with deep imposter syndrome. She didn't feel like the leader everyone thought she was.

She was torn between two identities: the professional woman in her 9 5 corporate job, and the aspiring entrepreneur trying to build something meaningful on the side. But in both spaces, she felt invisible. She was second-guessing every decision, over-apologizing, staying quiet in meetings, and constantly looking for external approval. Somewhere along the way, she had lost touch with who she really was.

The first thing I told her was, *"Before you can lead anyone else, you have to come back home to yourself."* So we didn't start with business strategy or leadership tactics. We started with **conviction**.

As her confidence coach, I helped her strip away the roles and expectations she felt pressured to perform in. We got clear on her values—what she stood for, what she wanted, and what she no longer had to tolerate. We identified the limiting beliefs that were fueling her imposter syndrome and reworked the narrative she had been telling herself for years.

I guided her through voice activation exercises so she could own her story and speak from a place of confidence, not fear. She practiced showing up unapologetically in meetings and setting boundaries in both her corporate job and her business. We reconnected her with her purpose and created a leadership identity that felt aligned—one that could live boldly in both spaces without compromise.

Within weeks, her energy shifted. She stopped shrinking. She started speaking up, leading with clarity, and trusting her instincts. Her team noticed. Her peers responded differently and most importantly, she responded differently. She no longer led to prove something. She led because she finally believed in who she was becoming.

That's the power of conviction. It doesn't make you louder. It makes you clearer. It makes you stronger.

It reminds you that you don't need a title to be impactful, you just need to lead from the inside out.

Conviction is Contagious

When you lead with conviction, you don't just change your direction—you change the energy in the room. People feel it before you speak. It's the way you walk into a space with purpose, the way your presence commands attention without needing to perform. Conviction shifts the atmosphere. It lets others know: this is a space where truth is welcome, where growth is possible, and where authenticity is safe.

Your conviction gives others permission to stop shrinking. It gives them courage to raise their hands, use their voices, and bring their full selves to the table. You become the mirror that reflects what's possible when someone leads from alignment instead of approval. When you're clear and grounded in who you are, others feel inspired to explore who they are too.

Conviction doesn't demand respect with noise or status—it commands it through presence and consistency. You don't have to bark orders or micromanage when your example speaks louder than your title. People follow leaders who are rooted. Leaders who mean what they say and live what they teach. Conviction isn't about control—it's about credibility.

Think back to the leaders who impacted your life most—maybe it was a teacher, a mentor, a manager, or a coach. Chances are, they weren't perfect. They didn't have all the answers. But they were anchored. They were steady. They were consistent. And because they were clear in their identity and values, they created space for you to rise. They made you believe that you could do more, be more, and lead more boldly just by the way they carried themselves.

That's the kind of leader conviction produces. Someone who isn't trying to impress, but trying to ignite. Someone who raises the bar just by showing up. Someone who transforms leadership from a burden into a blessing.

That's the power of conviction. It transforms leadership from obligation into opportunity. It shifts your mindset from *"I have to lead"* to *"I get to influence lives."* From *"I should"* to *"I'm called."*

The Confidence-Conviction Connection

You can't walk in alignment if you're constantly questioning your own voice. You can't influence others if deep down you're still shrinking in rooms you were built to stand tall in. Confidence isn't about being loud. It's about being grounded. It's knowing who you are—even when the room doesn't clap for you.

I've coached enough high-achieving women leaders and professionals to know this: most people don't lack skill—they lack *self-belief*. They have the experience, the education, the talent—but they're still doubting if they belong. That inner battle? It silently robs you of your power.

But here's what I want you to hear: Conviction doesn't come from perfection. It comes from alignment. From knowing what you carry. From trusting your assignment. From walking like the version of you that knows you are already equipped.

Rebuilding confidence isn't about being someone new. It's about remembering who you were *before* fear, burnout, or comparison made you forget. When you lead from that place, you're not just making moves—you're making an impact.

Because confident leaders don't perform—they show up. They don't need to dominate a room—they carry presence. They don't wait for permission—they walk in purpose.

So if you've been questioning yourself lately—hear me on this: You don't need more credentials to lead with conviction. You just need to believe that who you are *right now* is enough to get started.

Confidence is the fire. Conviction is the fuel. And when the two align—you don't just shift direction. You shift everything.

Final Thoughts

Leadership isn't about position, it's about posture. It's not about titles or applause. It's about how you show up when the room is quiet, the pressure is high, and the outcome is uncertain.

Leading with conviction means being rooted in who you are, even when the world tries to make you doubt it. It means leading yourself first—before the meetings, before the milestones, before the recognition. Because if you can't trust your own voice, you'll keep shrinking in rooms you were born to shift.

Conviction isn't just about what you say—it's how you move. It's the way you make decisions. The way you hold the line. The way you treat people and recover after falling short. It's not about perfection—it's about presence. The kind that says, I may not know everything, but I know I'm called. And I'm not backing down.

You don't need to wait for confidence to arrive before you lead. Confidence comes when you decide to lead anyway. You don't need to wait for validation. You validate yourself by the way you consistently show up and live out what you believe.

So whether you lead a team, a household, a business, a classroom—or just yourself—lead with conviction. Let your leadership reflect your values, your growth, and your truth. Be the kind of leader who doesn't just take up space—but shifts it. Because the most powerful leaders aren't always the loudest. They're the most anchored.

Action Steps

1. Define Your Conviction

Write down 3 core values that ground how you lead—in life, business, or relationships.

Ask yourself: What do I stand for, and how does my leadership reflect that?

2. Audit Your Alignment

Identify one area where you're currently leading from fear, people-pleasing, or performance.

What needs to shift so you can lead from alignment instead of approval?

3. Use Your Voice with Intention

Choose one moment this week to speak up with boldness.

Whether it's in a meeting, a conversation, or on social media—let your conviction lead your message.

4. Anchor Your Identity

Write a leadership affirmation that reflects who you are becoming.

Example: "I am a purpose-driven leader. I show up with clarity, courage, and conviction—even when it's uncomfortable." Say it aloud each morning this week.

Chapter 13:
Designing a Life of Purpose, Power, and Peace

There comes a time in your journey where survival is no longer enough. You've pushed through. You've endured. You've carried the weight of responsibilities, expectations, and pain that no one else saw—but deep down, you knew something had to change. You were done living on autopilot. Done performing for approval. Done carrying success that looked good on the outside but didn't feel good on the inside.

That was me.

I wasn't always walking in alignment. I've led major teams, carried high-level titles, delivered in corporate spaces, and checked every box that screamed "successful"—yet I still felt empty. I was managing a life, not living it. My smile was public, but my struggle was private. And then came the moment that changed everything: grief.

Losing my significant other shook me. Not just emotionally—but spiritually, mentally, and physically. I had to face life without the person who believed in me the most. I also had to face myself. I realized I had spent so long building my identity around doing, achieving, and serving everyone else that I had forgotten how to be with myself.

And that was just one layer.

I was also navigating burnout, the heaviness of leading others while feeling lost in my own vision, the pressure of being a minority woman in leadership, and the exhaustion of showing up strong when I was barely holding on. I knew how to lead others—but I had forgotten how to lead *me*.

So I made a decision. One that would shift everything:

I was going to rebuild my life—with intention.

I wasn't just going to survive—I was going to design a life that felt like home.

Rebuilding from Within

Designing a life of purpose, power, and peace didn't mean creating a perfect schedule, or getting everything right overnight. It meant doing the deep inner work to ask: *What do I want my life to feel like?*

Not just what do I want to do—but who do I want to be?

I had to let go of the version of me that was built in survival mode. I had to redefine success—not as hustle or overachievement, but as alignment, peace, and joy. I began to rebuild my days around what energized me, not what drained me. I started saying "no" to things that no longer served me, even if they used to define me.

And slowly, I found my rhythm again. I reclaimed my voice. I got clear on my calling. I created boundaries that protected my peace. I started living on purpose—not by default, but by design. This wasn't about escaping challenges. This was about meeting life with clarity and courage—about rising every day with intention and knowing that peace is not passive. When you've been knocked down by life—whether through grief, burnout, loss, or simply pretending to be someone you're not—what you crave most isn't just success. You crave substance. You want your life to feel whole again. Anchored. Intentional. Real. That's where *purpose, power,* and *peace* come in.

Purpose: The Anchor for Your Life

Purpose gives you life direction. It's your reason why. It answers the question: *What impact am I here to make?*

You don't find purpose by overthinking it. You find it by paying attention to what breaks your heart, what lights you up, and what calls you to action. Your purpose is often wrapped up in your story, your pain, your strengths, and your perspective.

My purpose didn't emerge in a high-powered meeting or a perfectly planned career move. It unfolded in the stillness—after the burnout, after the heartbreak, and after I felt completely disconnected from who I was and what I was doing. I used to believe that purpose was tied to a position or a paycheck. But I've learned that true purpose isn't found in your title—it's tied to your *calling*. It's about who you're meant to serve and how you're meant to show up. For me, that calling is clear: I'm here for the burnt-out leader who's forgotten their fire, the stuck professional trying to find direction, and the purpose-driven entrepreneur who has the vision but needs a strategy. I know those roles intimately, because I've lived every one of them—and I've had to rebuild from the inside out. That rebuilding started with confidence. Once I stopped performing and started believing in myself again, the fog lifted. The more confident I became, the clearer my purpose became. I no longer needed to chase significance—I was *anchored* in it.

Purpose isn't one moment or one milestone. It's a way of life. It's how you choose to lead, serve, speak, and show up when no one's applauding. Purpose is being intentional about the legacy you leave in every room, every conversation, and every role you step into. And when you begin to operate from purpose, everything shifts. You stop chasing outcomes, and you start honoring your assignment. That's when your life stops looking like survival—and starts feeling like alignment.

Power: Reclaiming Your Voice and Authority

Power isn't control—it's *ownership*. It's owning your identity, your story, your decisions, your boundaries, and your truth. It's standing in your worth without waiting for applause or approval. You don't need a title to be powerful. You don't need a stage or a following. You just need to *remember who you are* and take your power back from everything that convinced you to dim your light.

For years, I gave my power away. I over-explained, over-functioned, over-apologized. I silenced my ideas in meetings. I waited to be invited, to be validated, to be chosen. But here's the truth: **real power** doesn't wait to be chosen—it walks in already knowing it belongs.

And if you've ever felt overlooked in your 9–5, silenced in leadership, or unsure of your voice as a new entrepreneur—you're not alone. I've lived all three. I've been the high-achiever in corporate who quietly burned out trying to hold everything together. I've been the leader who looked the part but felt like an imposter. I've been the entrepreneur who launched with passion but lacked the confidence to be seen. And in every space, the breakthrough began when I reclaimed my authority—not just in business or leadership, but in *life*.

You reclaim your power when you:

- Set boundaries that protect your peace—not out of guilt, but out of self-respect.
- Make decisions that reflect your values, not your fears.
- Speak up even when your voice shakes—because silence is no longer serving your growth.
- Stop second-guessing your intuition and start trusting that the wisdom inside you is valid.

If you're a leader, a professional, or an entrepreneur who feels like you've lost your fire—it's time to return to the truth. You are not here to shrink. You are not here to beg for a seat at tables you've outgrown.

You are here to build, to rise, and to lead from a place of alignment and unapologetic authority.

This is the season to reclaim what burnout tried to break. This is your moment to remember that your voice *still matters* and when you lead from that place of power—doors open, clarity returns, and everything begins to shift. You stop living in reaction mode and start creating a life that reflects your authority.

Peace: The Fuel to Sustainable Growth

Let's be honest—if you're constantly running, overextending, and burning out behind the scenes, it doesn't matter how powerful your purpose is or how confident you look on the outside. Without peace, you'll eventually crash. And not because you're weak—but because you were never meant to build a meaningful life from a place of exhaustion.

Peace is not a luxury. Peace is fuel. It's what keeps you steady in the storm, focused in the noise, and grounded when life pulls you in ten directions. And for leaders, professionals, and entrepreneurs like us— peace is the foundation that holds everything else together.

I used to believe rest had to be earned. That if I wasn't producing, I wasn't progressing. But that mindset led me straight into burnout. I was leading in rooms I had prayed to be in—while silently unraveling inside. When I finally gave myself permission to slow down—to take a breath without guilt, to rest without needing to earn it, to say no without explaining myself—I began to experience peace in a way I never had before. Not the kind that just feels good for a moment, but the kind that anchors you. The kind that reminds you who you are when the world tries to make you forget. I used to believe rest would set me back. That pausing meant I was falling behind. But the moment I stopped running on autopilot and started honoring my own capacity, I realized something powerful: peace doesn't make you less productive—it makes you more *intentional*. It sharpens your focus, protects your energy, and strengthens your voice. That kind of peace made me a better leader, a clearer thinker, and a more present woman.

It didn't slow me down. It positioned me to rise—stronger, wiser, and fully aligned.

You create peace when you:

- Let go of roles, relationships, and routines that no longer serve your next level.
- Allow yourself to rest without performing or explaining.
- Say no with conviction and yes with alignment.
- Build stillness and spiritual grounding into your strategy—not just your recovery.

Peace isn't just a vibe—it's how you carry yourself when life applies pressure. It shows up in how you respond when things don't go as planned, in how you breathe through the tough calls, and in how your presence settles the room without needing to say a word. You know you're rooted in peace when you're no longer bracing for the next breakdown. Your nervous system isn't stuck in overdrive. You're not reacting out of fear—you're responding from a place of wholeness, clarity, and calm. That's when you know peace isn't just around you—it's in you. And from that place, you don't just move differently—you lead differently.

Peace doesn't mean life will be free of problems. It means you've built an internal foundation strong enough to withstand pressure without falling apart. It's the kind of strength that allows you to face challenges with clarity, navigate uncertainty with calm, and lead without losing yourself in the process.

When peace fuels your purpose and power, your growth becomes sustainable. You're no longer chasing results—you're moving from alignment. Your leadership gains presence, not just position. You don't have to overperform to be effective; your calm becomes your credibility.

You're not required to carry everything to prove you're strong. You don't have to do it all, hold it all, or wear the weight of constant striving. What you do need is the courage to choose a different way—to choose peace as your strategy, your pace, and your protection because the moment you let peace lead, everything else starts to align.

Peace is protective—it's a conscious decision to guard your mind, body, and spirit from chaos, distraction, and emotional overload. It's more than just silence or stepping away; peace is about *alignment*. It's the clarity that helps you lead with intention and the calm that keeps you grounded when everything around you feels loud. True peace isn't passive—it's powerful. It's the anchor that holds you steady and the filter that helps you discern what's worthy of your energy.

Integration: How It All Comes Together

You don't have to choose between purpose, power, and peace. You were designed to live in all three. When you align these elements, you become unstoppable.

- **Purpose** fuels your actions.
- **Power** gives you the confidence to carry them out.
- **Peace** sustains your capacity to do it long-term.

This is the new success. Not just working hard, but living well. Not just building empires, but nurturing your well-being. Not just rising in influence, but remaining rooted in integrity.

A Day in a Life of Alignment

Here's what life looks like when purpose, power, and peace are no longer competing—but working in harmony:

- You wake up grounded—not reacting to your schedule, but *owning* your time and setting the tone for your day.
- You make decisions from a place of clarity—not chaos, fear, or urgency.
- You honor your boundaries without apology—because your energy is too valuable to be constantly drained.

- You speak with confidence—not from a need to prove, but from a place of knowing your words carry weight.

- You end your day with fulfillment—not depletion—because what you gave came from a full cup, not from survival mode.

This life isn't just possible—it's *available*. And it's not reserved for the perfect, the privileged, or the polished. It's for the woman who's ready to stop striving and start living in alignment.

Purpose. Power. Peace. This is your new strategy. This is your new standard. And this is how you rise—with intention, clarity, and conviction.

Final Thoughts

You weren't called to build a life that impresses others but empties you. You were created to design a life that fuels your soul, supports your growth, and honors your divine assignment.Living in alignment means no longer choosing between purpose, power, and peace—but allowing all three to work together as the foundation of who you are and how you lead. When you move with purpose, you operate with clarity. When you reclaim your power, you lead with confidence. And when you protect your peace, you create space to grow without burning out. You weren't designed to live fragmented or exhausted—you were created to live whole, grounded, and intentional. This isn't about doing more—it's about becoming more aligned. And from that place, your life, leadership, and legacy can finally reflect the truth of who you are.

Action Steps

1. **Clarify Your Core Anchor Words**
   Write down one word that reflects how you want to live in each area:

   - My purpose is rooted in…

   - My power comes from…

   - My peace is protected by…

2. **Commit to One Alignment Shift This Week**
   What's one habit, decision, or conversation you've been avoiding that would bring you back into alignment? Do it.

3. **Create a Daily Reset Routine**
   Choose one thing you'll do each day to realign your mind, energy, or focus. (Examples: 10-minute meditation, 30 minute walk, journaling, boundaries check-in or writing down 3 things that you need to focus on that day that are non-negotiable.)

4. **Say this Declaration Out Loud Boldly - repeat it daily to serve as a friendly reminder**
   "I am a leader who lives with purpose, walks in my power, and protects my peace. I no longer shrink. I no longer perform. I rise—every single day—with clarity, confidence, courage, and conviction."

Your new chapter starts not with hustle, but with harmony.

Chapter 14:
Curating the Support You Need for Growth

Growth isn't meant to be a solo act. While personal transformation often begins in private—through self-reflection, hard choices, and quiet courage—it's sustained through connection. At some point in your journey, who surrounds you becomes just as important as the steps you take.

If you're serious about evolving, healing, rebuilding, or stepping into your purpose, you'll need to be just as intentional with your support system as you are with your goals. The people you allow into your space—whether it's your inner circle or a broader community—should reflect where you're going, not just where you've been.

Support is not a weakness. It's a strategy. It's what helps you stay aligned when distractions show up.

It's what reminds you who you are when life tries to make you forget. Whether you're launching a business, recovering from loss, leading a team, or rediscovering your voice, having the right support system—one that's aligned with your values, your mindset, and your mission—makes the difference between staying stuck and rising strong.

From Isolation to Alignment

I've always been independent—get-it-done, handle-it-myself energy. I thought strength meant doing it all alone. But after losing my partner and walking away from my career, I found myself on my knees.

That's when I realized: healing doesn't happen in isolation. Growth doesn't thrive in silence. I needed *support,* not just solitude.

I remember attending a women's empowerment event not long after my partner passed. I almost didn't go. I felt broken, empty, like I had nothing to offer. But something nudged me to show up. That night, I sat beside strangers who would become pivotal to my journey. One woman reached across the table, grabbed my hand, and said, "Your story is going to heal people."

I hadn't even shared a word of my story. But somehow, she saw something in me that I had buried beneath the grief, the burnout, and the silence. In that moment, her words pierced through the numbness and reached a part of me I didn't know was still alive. *She saw me—* not for who I was in that season, but for who I was still becoming.

That moment shifted something. It reminded me that when you place yourself in the right rooms, you don't have to prove your worth or perform your pain. The right people will recognize your powerEven when you've forgotten who you are, the right room will remember for you.

Growth Requires Support, Not Just Strength

One of the most damaging myths we're taught—especially in leadership and entrepreneurship—is that we always have to be the strong one. The one who carries the load, keeps it all together, and never shows a crack in the armor. But here's the truth most people won't say out loud: strength without support eventually leads to burnout, not breakthrough. No one rises to their next level alone.

You need people who:

- Challenge your blind spots
- Celebrate your wins
- Remind you of your worth
- Hold you accountable—with compassion, not control

Here's the truth that requires courage: some people simply won't be able to walk with you into your next season. They may have loved the version of you that stayed small, played safe, or kept the peace—but growth changes the dynamics. As you evolve, you'll quickly realize that not everyone is equipped to hold space for your expansion. Some connections were only aligned with your survival, not your success. And if you keep trying to bring everyone with you, you may end up shrinking to stay in spaces you've already outgrown. That's why curating your community isn't just a preference—it's necessary for your rise. Your next level demands more than strength. It calls for alignment, intentional support, and relationships that nurture who you're becoming—not just who you've been.

Letting Go to Grow Forward

There was a season when I felt stuck—like I was doing all the "right" things but still wasn't moving. It took me a while to realize that part of the reason was the company I was keeping. I was surrounded by people who were more connected to my past than committed to my growth. They weren't bad people—they just didn't grow with me.

When I started making bold moves—leaving a career that no longer fulfilled me, launching my business, stepping onto stages, and writing the book that had lived in my heart for years—I felt the shift. The energy changed. Conversations that used to feel light started to feel heavy. Some encouragement turned into subtle doubt. I realized I had outgrown the room, but I was still sitting in it—shrinking to stay connected.

That realization was painful, but it also became the turning point. I had to make the hard, necessary decision to lovingly create distance and welcome relationships that aligned with my purpose, my mindset, and where I was headed—not where I had been.

Once I began surrounding myself with purpose-driven, growth-minded, forward-focused people, everything shifted. My confidence deepened. My vision expanded. My fire returned.

Proximity is power. When you place yourself in the right rooms, your next level doesn't just feel possible—it becomes inevitable.

Signs It's Time to Shift Your Circle

- You feel dismissed or unsupported when you share your dreams.
- You leave conversations feeling drained or discouraged.
- You feel like you have to shrink, censor, or perform around certain people.
- You're always the one pouring, encouraging, or leading with no reciprocation.
- You second- guess your clarity after certain interactions.

Your circle should not compete with your clarity. It should confirm it.

Why Support Matters on the Growth Journey

The truth is, isolation might feel safe—but it often leads to stagnation. Especially in hard seasons, pulling away can feel like protection, but it actually shuts out the very support you need to rise. When you isolate, you silence the voices that could speak life into your purpose, clarity into your confusion, and strategy into your stuck moments.

Support systems—whether through personal relationships or intentional communities—are not luxuries, they are lifelines.

The right circle or community offers:

- **Perspective** when your vision becomes cloudy
- **Accountability** when your discipline starts to fade
- **Encouragement** when your confidence takes a hit
- **Opportunities** that you simply can't create on your own

When I stepped into entrepreneurship and embraced my calling as a speaker and coach, I knew I needed more than ambition—I needed alignment. So I made a decision: I was no longer going to build in silence. I joined masterminds, showed up to networking events, and surrounded myself with women who were walking in purpose. The more I leaned into intentional relationships, the more I realized something powerful: I didn't have to do this alone.

What a Growth-Aligned Support System Looks Like

A support system that matches your growth isn't built on convenience—it's built on *alignment*. It's about choosing to be surrounded by people who don't just see you, but who stretch you, sharpen you, and support the version of you that's still unfolding. It's not about cutting people off without reason—it's about protecting your energy, your momentum, and your mission.

There's a difference between **belonging to a community** and having an **intimate circle**—and both matter on the journey.

Your **community** is your collective—an empowering space of shared purpose, values, and energy. It might be your coaching group, a mastermind, or a room of dreamers and doers. Community gives you exposure, encouragement, new perspectives, and opportunities you wouldn't access alone. It reminds you that you're not the only one on this path—and that collective growth creates powerful momentum.

Your **circle**, however, is more personal. These are the trusted few who walk closely with you. The ones who check in on you, pray for you, speak truth to you, and hold space for your hard moments and honest questions. They see behind the scenes. They help you reset when the noise gets loud.

A growth-aligned support system includes **both**:

- A community that elevates your vision
- A circle that protects your heart

And here's the key—both aid in accountability, which is crucial to your personal growth journey. Your community challenges you to stay consistent with your calling, while your circle holds you to the standard you set for yourself. They help you realign when you drift, and remind you why you started when motivation fades.

This kind of support system becomes a safe space and a launchpad. It doesn't enable your excuses—it equips your evolution. The people in it won't let you shrink. They'll ask better questions, challenge your thinking, affirm your worth, and speak to the leader in you even when you don't feel like one.

Because when you're surrounded by people who are aligned with your growth, you don't just move forward—you rise stronger.

What to Look for in a Community

The right community is more than just a group of people—it's a mirror of your mission and a catalyst for your calling. It's a space where you don't have to shrink, perform, or constantly explain your vision. You're simply understood—and empowered.

Below are the key qualities to look for when choosing or creating a growth-aligned community:

Mutual Support

Everyone brings something to the table. In a thriving community, each person's goals, vision, and wellbeing matter. You support each other—not just with words, but with presence, ideas, and intentional action.

Accountability with Grace

Growth requires truth-tellers—people who lovingly challenge you without tearing you down. Real community doesn't let you settle. It helps you rise, with compassion at the center.

A Safe Space for Real Conversations

You can speak openly without fear of judgment, gossip, or your vulnerability being used against you. The right community creates room for honesty—not just highlight reels.

Celebration Without Jealousy

There's no silent competition—just genuine joy when someone wins. Their success doesn't diminish yours; it confirms what's possible for everyone.

Shared Vision or Values

You don't have to be identical, but there's alignment. Whether it's personal development, purpose-driven work, or becoming your best self—there's a shared language of growth and elevation.

When You Can't Find It—Create It

If you can't find the community you need—create it. That's what I did with the Convicted to Grow community. I wanted to be around leaders, dreamers, purpose-driven professionals who didn't just talk about goals, but actually did the work.

And now, every time I host a workshop or lead a group coaching call, I'm reminded: this is what alignment feels like. This is what it looks like to be in a community where everyone is rising, together.

So if you feel like you don't belong where you've been—that's your signal. You're not crazy. You're just called. And it's time to build or find the room that fits the future version of you.

When I started Convicted to Grow, it wasn't just about creating content or coaching clients. It was about building a space where people could come to be seen, heard, and challenged to rise. I saw how many aspiring leaders, coaches, and professionals were struggling—not because they lacked potential, but because they lacked support.

I wanted to change that. I knew firsthand what it felt like to rebuild from scratch, to doubt yourself, and to crave connection. That's why I made community a cornerstone of my brand. Because it's not just about what you know—it's about who walks with you.

Some of the most powerful breakthroughs in my journey didn't happen alone. They happened in community—in coaching calls, in collaborations, in deep conversations with people who reminded me of my greatness when I forgot.

I still remember one of our very first CTG live sessions. I watched as people shared their truth for the first time in a long time—raw, honest, and unfiltered. Tears were shed. Breakthroughs were born. And in that space, I knew this wasn't just a group—it was a movement. These were people ready to grow together. People ready to rise.

Final Thoughts

You deserve relationships that affirm your growth, not ones that leave you drained or doubting yourself. As you evolve, some connections will naturally shift—not because you've outgrown love, but because you've outgrown alignment. That's not rejection; it's redirection. Don't shrink to stay attached to people who only recognize the older version of you. Instead, be intentional about who surrounds you. Your next level may require a new room, new energy, and new support. You were never meant to grow alone—you were meant to rise with those who understand the journey. And if that circle doesn't exist yet, give yourself permission to build it. Start with you. Because your growth deserves good company—and so do you.

Action Steps

Growth doesn't just require strategy—it requires alignment. As you reflect on your support system, use these intentional steps to ensure your circle and community match where you're going, not just where you've been.

1. Evaluate Your Current Circle
Take a close look at the five people you interact with most. Do their mindset, energy, and conversations reflect the future you're building—or the version of you you've already outgrown?

2. Make Space

Growth requires room to breathe. Identify which relationships, patterns, or interactions need boundaries so you can protect your peace, focus, and momentum.

3. Seek Out Growth-Aligned Rooms

You don't have to do it alone—but you do need to be intentional about where you show up. Join private communities, groups from Facebook, LinkedIn as an example that align with your interests and values, stretch your thinking, and support your next level.

4. Be the Energy You Want to Attract

Lead with what you're looking for. Show up as the kind of friend, connector, and encourager you wish you had. The energy you give will begin to shape the energy you receive.

5. Speak It Into Existence

Use this affirmation daily to ground yourself in your intention:

"I am surrounded by people who inspire, uplift, and grow with me. I make room for alignment, not attachment."

Because growth deserves good company and you deserve a circle or community that matches your commitment for your next level greatness.

Chapter 15:
You Were Built for This

This is not the end of your story. It's the beginning of the version of you that doesn't flinch when storms come. The version of you that doesn't wait to feel ready. The version of you that knows—deep in your gut—you were built for this.

I didn't always know that about myself. There was a time I felt like life had completely unraveled. I had checked every box: successful career, leadership role, six-figure income and in a relationship, but I was burned out, broken, and barely holding myself together behind the smile. And then grief knocked on my door—uninvited, unexpected, and unapologetic. The unexpected loss of my significant other cracked me wide open. I wasn't sure how to breathe, let alone rebuild. I questioned everything: my direction, my identity, my ability to lead, and whether I had the strength to start over.

In the quiet of that pain, I heard a whisper: *You were built for more.*

But here's what I learned: purpose doesn't go away when pain shows up. I had a purpose to finish what I started. Yes, I went through setbacks. Yes, I struggled with navigating challenges and losing myself but that is where my resilience was developed. My delay in my purpose wasn't a mistake. It was divine timing. I had to go through the process in order to get to the promise.

Rebuilding isn't glamorous. It's gut-wrenching, vulnerable work. It's waking up every day and choosing to believe that who you're becoming is worth fighting for. And when I was at my lowest, I had to look in the mirror and ask myself a hard question: Are you going to stay here, or are you going to rise?

Rebuilding is rawl, real and sometimes uncomfortable. There were days I barely recognized myself. But that's the thing about transformation—it doesn't ask for your comfort. It asks for your *commitment*. The decision to stop surviving and start living intentionally required more than vision; it required conviction.

Maybe you're in that place right now—where everything familiar has shifted, where what once made sense no longer fits. You're carrying silent pressure to "figure it out" while still holding it together for everyone else. You're navigating silent battles nobody sees. But guess what . you're still standing. You're still breathing.But deep down, you feel it... this nudge that won't go away. That whisper reminding you: *You were made for more.*

So let me say this to you directly:
You were not built to shrink in rooms that need your presence.
You were not built to settle for less.

You were not built to carry dead weight, dim your light, or delay your dreams.

You were built to lead with confidence and clarity.
You were built to be resilient without losing yourself.
You were built to go through it in order to grow.
You were built to rise stronger!

Every chapter of your life you've walked through—every loss, every lesson, every time you had to start over—was preparing you for the next level in which your life doesn't require perfection. It requires ownership.

Those who rise with conviction don't wait for permission. They trust the call on their life and lean into it. They build, even when no one is clapping. They show up, not because they feel ready, but because they remember who they are. Because when you rise, you don't rise alone. You make room for others to rise with you.

Everything you've faced—every transition, setback, or start-over—was shaping your strength. You weren't buried. You were being prepared. Now it's time to stop questioning the calling and start owning it.

There's someone out there waiting on the version of you that shows up fully. Someone who needs your story, your voice, your strategy, your truth. That's the power of living with conviction—it doesn't just change your life, it creates a ripple effect that reaches further than you can imagine.

The person you are becoming will open doors, shift atmospheres, and inspire others to grow. That's not hype—it's true. You were built for this.

Rebuilding Confidence: The Journey Back to You

Rebuilding confidence isn't about becoming someone new—it's about *returning to who you were before the world told you to shrink.* It's peeling back the layers of fear, burnout, doubt, and disappointment to reconnect with the version of you that still believes, still hopes, and still dreams. After my own unraveling—grief, career burnout, and an identity crisis that left me questioning everything—I realized confidence doesn't come from titles or applause. It comes from doing the inner work. From trusting your voice again. From standing in rooms where your knees may shake, but you speak anyway. Rebuilding confidence means making peace with where you've been while boldly claiming where you're going. It's not a quick fix—it's a powerful decision to rise, again and again, until you see yourself clearly and walk with conviction.

The Pause Is Part of the Process

For so long, I thought slowing down meant I was falling behind. I believed that if I wasn't producing, performing, or pushing forward, I was somehow losing momentum. I was wired to move—always planning, always pouring, always showing up for everything and everyone. Slowing down felt like failure in a world that glorifies hustle. But when life knocked the wind out of me—when grief hit, when burnout caught up, when clarity felt miles away—I didn't need another to-do list. I needed a moment to *breathe.*

At first, the pause felt like punishment. It was uncomfortable to sit in silence without a plan or a path. But that stillness became a mirror. It revealed the weight I had been carrying for far too long, the parts of myself I had ignored, and the healing I had pushed to the side while I kept performing like everything was fine. What I once viewed as a setback eventually became sacred space—because the pause gave me permission to reconnect with who I was beyond the title, the role, or the routine.

I had to learn that growth doesn't always look like movement. Sometimes the most powerful transformation happens when everything slows down—when you catch your breath, confront your truth, and give yourself grace to be human. Confidence isn't only built in doing; it's cultivated in those quiet moments when you're finally still enough to hear yourself think, reflect, and realign.

So if you're in a season where things feel quiet, unclear, or even paused, don't rush to escape it. That pause is preparing you. It's making space for clarity. It's stretching your capacity. It's helping you rebuild, not just on the surface, but at your core. You're not falling behind—you're being repositioned for what's next. Honor the pause, because it's not the end of your progress; it's where the real rebuilding begins.

What Does Your Next Level Look Like?

For a long time, I thought my next level had to look like a title, a salary bump, or a picture-perfect plan. But after losing someone I loved and walking away from a career that no longer aligned with who I was becoming, I realized the next level isn't always something you climb to—it's something you *grow into.* My next level looked like giving myself permission to slow down, to heal, to rebuild without a blueprint, and to speak life back into a version of me I had buried under expectations. Maybe your next level doesn't look like what you imagined either—and that's okay. It might look like reclaiming your confidence, starting something new even if your hands are shaking, or finally putting yourself first. Don't wait for everything to make sense before you move. Your next level isn't a destination—it's a decision. A choice to believe that who you're becoming is worth showing up for, again and again. You've already made it through the hard part. Now it's time to rise like you were built to.

The Conviction to Keep Rising

There comes a moment when motivation fades, clarity gets cloudy, and life tests everything you said you were ready for—and it's in that moment where conviction has to kick in. I remember waking up one morning, months after leaving my career, and asking myself, *"What am I even doing?"* The grief was still heavy. The vision wasn't fully clear. The bank account didn't match the dream. But deep down, I knew something had shifted—I wasn't rising because I felt confident. I was rising because I was convicted. Convicted that my life had more meaning. That my voice had value. That my journey wasn't over. That kind of conviction doesn't come from hype—it comes from *truth.* From remembering who you are and who you've survived becoming. So if you're feeling tired or questioning your steps, let this be your reminder: your rise isn't about being perfect or prepared. It's about being committed. Don't stop now. You didn't come this far to shrink. You've got too much purpose left in you. Keep rising—because your next level is waiting on your *yes.*

Final Thoughts

Listen—this isn't about starting over. This is about starting *stronger.* Everything you've walked through has built something in you. That strength? That resilience? That's your foundation now. Rebuilding your confidence isn't a one-time moment—it's a daily decision to show up for yourself, even when the voice of doubt tries to talk louder than your purpose. You're not behind. You're becoming. You've already survived what was meant to break you, and now it's time to rise with clarity, conviction, and confidence. The next version of you doesn't need permission—just alignment. Keep going. You were built for this, and your growth is not just personal—it's *powerful and it's a daily thing! WE ARE ON THIS GROWTH JOURNEY TOGETHER and Yes, I am rooting for you!*

You've read the book.. You've felt the pull. But growth doesn't stop here—it continues in your next move.

Action Steps

1. **Write a Letter to Your Future Self**
   Describe who you are a year from now. Visualize your success. Speak to the bold, confident, purposeful version of you. What are you doing? How are you living?

2. **Create a Built-For-This List**
   Write down five hard things you've overcome. Remind yourself of your strength.

3. **Declare It Out Loud:**
   "I was built for this. I am not who I used to be. I lead, live, and grow with confidence and conviction."

4. **Reflect on Your Journey**
   Reread past journal entries, notes, or moments of doubt. Celebrate your growth.

5. **Take the Next Bold Step**
   Whatever has been on your heart—start it. Say yes. Move forward. You're ready.

This may be the end of the chapter, but it's just the beginning of the becoming—your journey of being Convicted to Grow.

You've read the lessons. You've felt the shifts. Now it's time to walk in it. Because you weren't just meant to survive—you were built to lead, to rise, and to grow. Your next chapter starts now. Let's go!

Closing

Bonus Chapter:
The Convicted Framework

Convicted to Grow wasn't just a cute name for a book or a brand. It was birthed in the middle of my pain. It came to life during the days when I questioned everything — my worth, my voice, my calling. But what started as a whisper from God became the anthem I chose to live by.

This chapter is for that version of you that's still doubting, still holding on, still afraid to let go of what broke you. This is the part where you stop repeating old cycles — and start rewriting the narrative.

This is your code to rebuild, not just once, but every time life tries to knock the wind out of you. Let me introduce you to the C.O.N.V.I.C.T.E.D. Framework — your personal guide for rising, growing, and leading with bold, unshakable confidence.

The Confidence Rebuild Code That Will Elevate Your Next Season

C – Clarity

You cannot rise in confusion. Growth begins the moment you get honest about who you are, what you value, and where you're headed.

Reflection Prompt: What's one belief you need to release in order to see yourself clearly again?

O – Ownership

This is about taking your power back. Your story is yours. Your voice is yours. You don't need permission to own your healing.

Exercise: Write down 3 things you are no longer apologizing for. Say them aloud and mean every word.

N – New Identity

You're not who you used to be — and that's a good thing. Titles, trauma, and timelines don't define you. This is your rebirth.

Prompt: Describe yourself without listing a job title, role, or label. Who are you becoming?

V – Voice Activation

Your voice carries weight. Power. Authority. It's not meant to be silenced. Speak up, even if it shakes at first.

Try This: Choose one truth you've been holding back — something you've been afraid to say out loud. Speak it into a voice note, journal it with boldness, or say it to someone you trust. Let your voice lead your healing, not your silence.

I – Inner Work

This is where confidence is really built — in the quiet, in the tears, in the prayers. When no one's watching, that's where the healing happens. Confidence isn't built in performance mode. It's built in private.

Self-Check: What belief or behavior are you actively working to unlearn right now? What's one intentional habit you can practice right now to stay aligned with the version of you that's already growing?

C – Confidence

Confidence isn't about being loud. It's about being rooted. It's about choosing to show up — even when your voice shakes.

Challenge: For the next 7 days, show up boldly in one area of your life. Choose presence over perfection.

T – Transformation

You didn't just survive — you've evolved. The old you would be so proud of how far you've come. Now walk like you know it.

Journal Prompt: What version of you have you outgrown? Who are you becoming in this new season?

E – Elevation

You weren't meant to stay where you fell. Your setback was never your ceiling — it was preparation. Every challenge, every loss, every delay? It was building something in you that comfort never could. Now it's time to rise — with vision, with intention, and with clarity about the future you're stepping into.

Exercise: Create a digital or physical vision board for the *elevated version of you*. Don't just make it pretty — make it personal and aligned. Include images, words, and symbols that reflect what you're calling in across every dimension of your life:

- **Life & Lifestyle:** How do you wake up, move, and show up each day?
- **Career or Business:** What does impact, influence, and fulfillment look like at your next level?
- **Finances:** What are you earning, managing, or investing in with confidence and wisdom?
- **Health & Wellness:** How does your body feel? How are you nurturing your energy, not just your productivity?
- **Relationships:** Who are you surrounded by? What kind of love, connection, and community are you building?

Next Step:

Once your vision board is complete, give this next season a name. Speak it over yourself. Write it on a sticky note. Use it as your anchor.

Because what you visualize consistently, you begin to align with daily.

D – Drive

Growth without direction leads to burnout. You've rebuilt, now it's time to move forward with purpose. Drive is your daily decision to keep going — not just for success, but for alignment, fulfillment, and impact.

Final Reflection: What's fueling your drive right now — fear or purpose? How can you shift your actions to reflect where you're going, not just what you've been through?

Conclusion:
Your Convicted to Grow Blueprint

L et me be real with you—writing this book wasn't easy. Just like the process it describes, it stretched me. It forced me to go back and sit in moments I would've rather skipped over. I had to relive some things I never thought I'd share publicly. But I knew if I was going to truly walk in my purpose—and help you do the same—I couldn't hold back. That is what Convicted to Grow is all about.

When I lost my significant other suddenly and walked away from a career that no longer served me, I didn't feel strong. I didn't feel "called." I felt lost. Grief and burnout had me questioning my worth, my direction, and honestly, my future. But somewhere in that stillness, I heard something rise up in me—a conviction. A quiet but firm reminder: *You were built for this.*

Not just the success. Not just the spotlight. But the healing. The hard work. The rebuilding.

That's where *Convicted to Grow* was born—from the ashes of who I used to be, into the bold, faith-filled, purpose-driven woman I'm still becoming. This isn't about being perfect. It's about being *real* with yourself. About being honest about what broke you, what shaped you, and what's still pulling you forward.

This book is more than chapters—it's a reflection of your own rise. It's your journey in real time, unfolding page by page, moment by moment, truth by truth. You walked through **The Fall**, not just reading about setbacks but reliving the ones that left you questioning everything. You felt the heaviness of grief, the pain of transitions, the fear of being stuck in a version of yourself that no longer fit. You've known what it's like to smile on the outside while silently breaking down on the inside. That part of the journey taught you how to be honest—with yourself and with your reality.

Then came **The Rebuild**, where nothing looked perfect, but everything mattered. That's where you started to gather the broken pieces and ask yourself, *Who am I now?* You stopped performing and started healing. You gave yourself permission to let go of who you had to be and began choosing who you were ready to become. Rebuilding requires you to release old versions of yourself, unlearn survival mode, and choose alignment over approval.

In **The Rise**, you made a decision—even if your knees were shaking—to stand. Maybe you didn't feel fully ready, but you chose to show up anyway. You began to reclaim your confidence, to speak with more courage, to move with more intention. The Rise wasn't about having it all figured out—it was about remembering that your voice has power and your presence has purpose.

And now here we are in **The Commitment**—the part most people skip. This is where the habits are formed. This is where the mindset shifts take root. This is where you no longer grow out of desperation, but from *discipline*. This part isn't just about bouncing back—it's about building forward. You're no longer trying to prove anything. You're living it. Embodying it. You're becoming someone who doesn't just talk about confidence—you *live* with it. You lead with it. You carry it into every room you walk into.

Because this journey isn't just about healing from the past—it's about holding yourself accountable to the future you've been praying for.

What Convicted to Grow Really Means

Convicted to Grow isn't just a phrase—it's a declaration. A decision. A mindset. A movement.

It was born during one of the darkest seasons of my life, when everything I thought was secure fell apart. I had the career. The income. The title. But behind the scenes, I was exhausted. I was grieving. I was questioning my purpose, my identity, and whether I had anything left to give. When I lost my significant other, it broke something in me—but it also woke something up. I realized I couldn't keep living in survival mode, performing for the world while feeling empty inside.

That was the moment I got *convicted*—not in guilt, but in truth.

Convicted that I was created for more.
Convicted that my healing mattered.
Convicted that playing small was no longer an option.
Convicted that growth wasn't a luxury—it was a requirement.

To be *Convicted to Grow* means you refuse to go back to who you had to be just to keep it together. It means you're no longer led by fear, but by alignment. You no longer wait to be chosen—you choose yourself. It's about holding your head high, even when your heart is still healing. It's about showing up before you feel fully ready, because your purpose can't afford to wait.

Growth isn't just something that happens to you—it's something you *commit* to. Daily. Boldly. Intentionally. You grow through the discomfort. Through the doubt. Through the in-between. You grow because your future depends on it.

This movement isn't about perfection or performance—it's about *permission*. Permission to evolve. Permission to reset. Permission to lead, live, and love from a deeper place of truth. *Convicted to Grow* is about becoming someone who owns their story, walks in confidence, and creates impact—not in spite of the hard things, but *because of them.*

So when you say you're *Convicted to Grow*, you're not just speaking a brand...

You're owning a blueprint.
You're building a legacy.
You're rising in your power.
You're becoming who you were always meant to be.

This isn't just a personal mantra—it's a lifelong commitment.

That's what *Convicted to Grow* really means. It means being so rooted in who you're becoming that you refuse to go back to who you had to be. It's about moving differently because you know better now. It's trusting that you don't need more time—you need more truth. More alignment. More community. More confidence in the person staring back at you in the mirror.

That's what *Convicted to Grow* is all about.

It's not just a brand. It's a way of life. It's the decision to rise *again and again*, to lead yourself with intention, and to show up for your purpose—even when it's uncomfortable, even when it costs you something, even when it means starting over.

You've now got the blueprint:

- **Acknowledge the Fall**: Be honest about where you've been.
- **Choose to Rebuild**: Give yourself grace and strategy to grow.
- **Step Into the Rise**: Own your story, your voice, and your power.
- **Commit to Growth**: Don't just talk about it—*live it*.

Let's Grow—Together

Growth isn't a solo mission—and you don't have to figure it out alone. If this book spoke to something deep inside of you, then consider it your invitation to take the next step with me.

Join the **Convicted to Grow Community** at ctgcommunity.com—a space where we grow in confidence, strategy, purpose, and presence, together. You'll gain access to live coaching, accountability, resources, and a support system that *gets it*—because they're walking the same path too.

Or if you're ready for deeper, personalized transformation and want to work with me 1:1 coaching, visit convictedtogrow.com and let's talk about your goals, your vision, and how we can get you moving with clarity and confidence.

Whether you're rebuilding from a setback, launching something new, or simply choosing to rise differently this time—I want you to know this:

- You were *never* behind. You were just being positioned.
- You were *never* too late. You were being prepared.
- You were *always* built for this.
- And I'm rooting for you every step of the way.
- You are Convicted to Grow in every area of your life!

Reader's Reflection Journal

This section is your space. You've just completed a transformational journey through the pages of this book, and now it's time to process, reflect, and commit to continued growth. Use the following prompts to go deeper, revisit key lessons, and turn insights into action. Write your answers in your Convicted to Grow Notebook.

Reflection Prompts

1. **What was your personal "conviction moment" while reading this book?**
   Describe a moment or quote that stopped you in your tracks and made you think differently.

2. **Which chapter resonated the most with you—and why?**
   What part of your life or mindset does it speak to?

3. **What limiting beliefs did you identify and begin to release during this journey?**
   How are you choosing to rewrite the narrative?

4. **What does confidence mean to you now, and how has that definition shifted?**
   Write a new, empowered definition of confidence in your own words.

5. **What are three things you are no longer available for in your life, career, or business?**
   Be bold. Be honest.

6. **What new habits, mindsets, or routines will you commit to moving forward?**

   List 1–3 shifts you're ready to embody daily.

7. **What is one fear you're finally ready to confront—and how will you take the first step?**

   Courage isn't the absence of fear, it's moving anyway.

8. **Who do you need to become to walk in alignment with your purpose?**

   Describe her/him/them in detail. What do they believe, say, and do?

9. **How will you use your voice and story to empower others?**

   Your healing has ripple effects. Who needs to hear your truth?

10. **What's your personal mantra or affirmation after reading this book?**

    Write one that you can return to whenever you need a reminder of who you are.

Take this section seriously. Growth happens when you pause, reflect, and realign.

Convicted to Grow Affirmations

These aren't just affirmations—they're convictions. Truths you can speak over your life as you rebuild your confidence and rise stronger. These words are here to help you shift your mindset, reset your energy, and stay grounded in who you're becoming.

How to Use This Section:

- Read through each affirmation slowly and reflect on how it speaks to your current season.

- **Pick 3–5 statements** that resonate with your heart, healing, or goals.

- **Highlight them** and make them part of your morning routine.

- Speak them out loud daily—with boldness, clarity, and belief—until they no longer feel like just words, but your truth.

Rebuild

1. I am allowed to start over—and this time, I'm building with purpose.
2. I honor who I used to be, but I'm no longer defined by who I was.
3. My healing is not a setback—it's the setup for my next level.
4. I trust the process, even when it's uncomfortable.
5. I don't need to have it all figured out to take the first step.

Resilience

6. I am not broken—I am rebuilding with strength and clarity.

7. Every challenge I've faced has prepared me for this season.

8. I rise every time I realign, not just when I'm perfect.

9. I give myself grace to grow through what I go through.

10. I may bend, but I do not break—I bounce back stronger.

Confidence

11. I am worthy, even when I feel uncertain.

12. I speak with clarity, courage, and conviction.

13. Confidence is not perfection—it's presence and permission to be me.

14. My voice matters. My story matters. *I* matter.

15. I no longer shrink to fit— I expand to lead.

Clarity & Purpose

16. I am in alignment with who I'm becoming.

17. I don't chase— I attract what's meant for me through alignment.

18. I am clear on my mission and bold in my message.

19. I choose purpose over pressure.

20. My past doesn't disqualify me— it fuels my calling.

Growth & Elevation

21. I am not behind—I'm being prepared.

22. Growth isn't always loud. Even in stillness, I am becoming.

23. I celebrate every step, even the small ones.

24. I no longer wait for permission to rise.

25. I was convicted to grow—and I choose to rise stronger every day.

Next Steps:
Your Invitation to Keep Rising

If this book impacted you, know this: your journey is far from over. The work you've begun here is just the start of an even greater transformation.

Here's how you can stay connected, supported, and equipped:

1. Join the CTG Circle Community - <u>ctgcommunity.com</u>

This is your hub for coaching, collaboration, confidence-building, and growth. Join other professionals, leaders, and entrepreneurs who are committed to living out their next level. Expect weekly coaching and strategy sessions, quarterly challenges, exclusive trainings, networking opportunities, and more.

2. Work with Me - <u>convictedtogrowcoaching.com</u>

If you're ready to elevate your brand, build confidence in your voice, or step boldly into the next chapter of your life or business—I'd love to support you. Explore one of my programs or invite me to speak at your next event, workshop, or organization.

3. Share the Movement

Post a photo of your book, a favorite quote, or your reflection on social media using #ConvictedToGrow. Let others know that they don't have to grow alone. Tag me @coachtressa

4. Lead a Book Club or Group

This book was designed for conversation. Use the journal prompts and chapter takeaways to lead others through the same growth process. Leadership starts with you.

5. Stay Inspired

Subscribe to the YouTube channel @Convicted to Grow , follow me on IG and Tik Tok @CoachTressa for weekly encouragement, inspiration, and behind-the-scenes insight as I continue to grow alongside you.

Your next level isn't waiting—it's already calling. You've been equipped. You've been prepared. And now, you rise.

Let's grow together. Let's lead with conviction.

If you would like to place a bulk order for your group- email info@tressamanns.com for discounted pricing or go to www.convictedtogrow.com

www.ingramcontent.com/pod-product-compliance
Lightning Source LLC
Chambersburg PA
CBHW071753120626
46550CB00002B/777